The LEEDS & WEST YORKSHIRE Cook Book

A celebration of the amazing food & drink on our doorstep.
Featuring over 35 stunning recipes.

The Leeds & West Yorkshire Cook Book

©2016 Meze Publishing. All rights reserved.

First edition printed in 2016 in the UK.

ISBN: 978-1-910863-18-3

Thank you to: Simon & Rena Gueller, The Box Tree

Compiled by: Lisa Pullen

Written by: Kate Reeves-Brown, Kerre Chen,
Kelsie Marsden, Rachel Heward

Photography by: Tim Green
(www.timgreenphotographer.co.uk)

Edited by: Phil Turner

Designed by: Matt Crowder, Paul Cocker,
Marc Barker

PR: Kerre Chen

Cover art: Luke Prest (www.lukeprest.com)

Contributors: Sarah Koriba

Published by Meze Publishing Limited
Unit S8 & S9 Global Works
Penistone Road
Sheffield S6 3AE
Web: www.mezepublishing.co.uk
Tel: 0114 275 7709
Email: info@mezepublishing.co.uk

Printed by Bell & Bain Ltd, Glasgow

FOREWORD

From sophisticated fine dining and quirky independent cafés to classic pub grub and country farm shops, Leeds and West Yorkshire has a thriving food scene. Great food starts with great produce and the rolling moors of this county are alive with some of the best...

We are so lucky in Yorkshire, being such a huge county there's so much to go at for food lovers, the variety of cuisines on offer is staggering! When we can, we take a drive out in to the dales to some of the cosy country pubs or if we stay in town Rena's favourite is a local Vietnamese restaurant. Whilst there are a lot of chain restaurants in the area, we feel it's really important to keep supporting the local independent restaurants , that's where we find some of the best food and a more personal service.

The county has been good to us and we have a very long history here, before taking on The Box Tree we opened Rascasse in Leeds city centre, which went on to gain its first Michelin star within a year in 1996. Since then we have continued to be a driving force on the restaurant scene in Yorkshire, focusing on improving and retaining the quality of food and service. Where possible we try to source locally and seasonally grown food which isn't too hard as we have some of the UK's best food producers right on our doorstep.

We have well established relationships with customers and suppliers spanning over almost 30 years. We are very passionate about upholding the heritage of The Box Tree and its long standing reputation in the area by creating a warm, comfortable, relaxed atmosphere, delivering great food and great service. In addition to this our award-winning outside catering company Box Tree Events handles private, corporate and wedding functions as well as the catering at some of Yorkshires finest stately homes for example Harewood House and Denton Hall.

Whilst all this keeps us very busy its still great to get out and about and explore the food scene and what's going on in the area its always evolving with new styles and flavours which keeps us all on our toes.

Whether you use this book to read about the wonderful places and people featured in it or to find your new favourite recipe, just have fun and enjoy it!

Simon and Rena Gueller

Chef proprietor and managing director at The Box Tree restaurant

CONTENTS

Leeds through
THE LENS

Leeds-born photographer Tim Green has photographed more than 30 cook books to date, so bringing his home city's food scene to life in this book has been a dream come true.

Tim Green first began his career in photography in a studio in Hunslet in Leeds. Born into a family of butchers, he had grown up surrounded by an appreciation for food. Despite deciding to embark on a career as a photographer, it wasn't long before food became the focus of his work too.

Early in his career Tim worked for a renowned jazz photographer Terry Cryer. This was before the food revolution had begun and Leeds wasn't jam-packed with the plethora of amazing places to eat like it is today. However, Terry introduced him to the amazing hidden gems of the city, showing him just how incredible food could be. Tim developed an appreciation of good cooking and creative cuisine, and still remembers Terry's role in opening his eyes to the world of food as well as inspiring his photography career.

Tim has experienced an impressive career so far, having worked with Meze Publishing since the company was founded. He loves capturing food through the lens. He explains what makes food photography such a special experience for him:

"I love food, but I also like the creativity of shooting food. Chefs are so visual when it comes to their dishes – they taste amazing but they also look incredible. I enjoy being able to work with the light, angles and composition to really capture the dish. It's a really creative process for everyone involved."

He has been lucky enough to work with a whole range of people from street food traders to acclaimed chefs, and he finds them all equally inspiring. "I have been lucky enough to travel to far-flung places, such as Thailand, to shoot food. I have met so many people all doing really inspiring things. From people cooking incredible dishes from the back of a tiny trailer to Michelin-star chefs."

He loves that each client is unique and every shoot is a new adventure. Meeting new people and hearing their stories is one of the things that makes him tick, and he is always on the lookout for new people to work with, new stories to be inspired by and new tastes to experience.

www.timgreenphotographer.co.uk

A history of four GENERATIONS

Bolster Moor Farm Shop in Huddersfield is a prime example
of a true thriving family business.

Bolster Moor Farm Shop is owned and run by Simon Haigh and Andrew Whitwam, who are second cousins. Together they are driven by carving out a path for the future generation – they have six boys between them.

Today, the two eldest members of the fourth generation are involved as butcher and farmer, with their mums also playing key roles in the running of the business. In fact, Simon's son Luke represented England in 2011 at the Young Butcher competition at just 20 years old – a chip off the old block!

The family's hard work has seen the business go from strength to strength, whilst still sitting on the site of the old family farm – something the family know would have made great grandad extremely proud. Bolster Moor sits 328 metres above sea level, with far reaching countryside views. The farm shop has become the hub of it's village community, yet also has customers flocking from far and wide.

Butchers by trade, Simon and Andrew are still very much hands-on at the counter. It's something of a spectacle to watch the large butchery team at work, who are just as good at Yorkshire banter as they are at craft butchery. Cooking tips are given willingly and a joke is shared cheerfully. It's all about good old-fashioned service – nothing is too much trouble. The fresh meat attracts chefs from some of the finest eateries in the area, including the renowned Three Acres Inn.

Plus, there's an on-site bakery, dedicated pie team and grocery. To make the trip even more worthwhile, there's also a gem of a coffee shop, providing a cosy retreat in winter and fantastic al-fresco eating in summer. Here they serve delicious farm shop produce, all-day breakfasts and the famous bacon sandwiches that were awarded 'Britain's Best Bacon Butty' by BBC Olive Magazine. They've even got a little seasonal magazine to browse whilst you eat, packed with recipes and more of that Yorkshire banter…

Some 3500 championship pork pies are made and sold each week. In fact the pies are so good that there is a demand for their unique three-tier pork pie wedding cakes! Add that to the 1.5 tonnes of fresh championship sausages that are made weekly, in many different varieties and the 15,000 bread teacakes they bake each week, there is never a quiet day at Bolster Moor Farm Shop.

WELCOME TO

BOLSTER MOOR FARM SHOP

Farmers AT HEART

Family, heritage and their farming roots are at the heart of everything at Bolster Moor Farm Shop.

The farm at Bolster Moor has been in the family since 1953 when it was bought by Simon's grandfather and subsequently passed down through the family. Simon and Andrew grew up helping on the farm and trained as butchers on leaving school. Together they have a collective butchery experience of 50 years and their dream of opening Bolster Moor Farm Shop was realised in 2009.

Today there is still a direct connection kept between the farm and the farm shop. The farm has more than 200 cross-bred cattle for meat, plus 115 breeding ewes, which are cross-bred Texels, and a few pedigree Aberdeen Angus cattle. Everything that is farmed comes through the farm shop.

To this end, most of the beef and lamb at Bolster Moor Farm Shop is their own. Where they need to bolster their own stocks, they source from local farms and in doing so help the local farming community. The pork comes from a piggery within the village and the poultry from a farm in Golcar, less than two miles away. The ethos 'local is best' resonates strongly at Bolster Moor Farm Shop.

It's evident too that the farming gene prevails in this family, with Simon's son Jack in charge of the livestock. Andrew's children are still of school age, but his middle son Lewis spends every spare moment on the farm helping out – another young farmer in the making, taking the family farm story into the fourth generation.

Simon Haigh comments: "We're very proud to be doing what we do on the site of my grandfather's farm, it means that we continue what he started all those years ago in this beautiful corner of Yorkshire. I feel very lucky to hail from here and I wouldn't want to live anywhere else."

Our bangers are the best in the UK

The PIE MASTERS

Championship-standard pies made to a secret recipe... the family's pork pies have achieved something of a legendary reputation in the area.

Simon and Andrew have been making pork pies throughout their careers and have perfected the recipe over the years. The dedicated pie team makes the pies to championship standard, using a secret recipe. They start early in the morning before the farm shop opens, so that there are freshly baked pies daily for customers.

Andrew Whitwam comments: "The success of a champion pork pie for us is that it's made using well-sourced ingredients and a nice thin crust. The meat is cured first to give it that distinctive pink colour and to give a nice even texture, which is the regional preference in our area."

This pie mastery has been rewarded with countless accolades and most recently their traditional pork pie was awarded 'The World's Best Pork Pie' at the Pork Pie Appreciation Society competition. In fact, it's the seventh time they've taken the award!

They made history in winning every trophy going at The Great Yorkshire Pork Pie & Sausage Competition for their pork pies and different varieties of sausage. All these trophies, plus the ones awarded for their sausages, are on display in the farm shop – the team admit they are going to need a bigger trophy shelf very soon.

The pies are so popular (apparently they have been known to make grown Yorkshire men squeal with delight), it's no joke that their delivery van says 'no pies left in this van overnight'. The big question is... are they best enjoyed with red sauce or brown? It's a very controversial issue around Bolster Moor Farm and of course one that only you can decide.

Alternatively, a champion traditional pork pie can be enjoyed in Bolster Moor Coffee Shop, served warm with a generous portion of their homemade ham hock mushy pies... Yorkshire on a plate.

SPROUTS
£1·20kg

Bolster Moor Farm Shop
BEEF BOURGUIGNON PIE

This recipe uses Bolster Moor Farm Shop feather blade steak and adds a novel twist by turning a French classic into a crowd-pleasing pie. It fills the house with a beautiful smell when it's in the oven!

Preparation time: Approx. 30 minutes | Cooking time: Approx. 3 hours | Serves: 4

Ingredients

800g Bolster Moor feather blade steak, cut into large chunks

Plain flour, seasoned

5 tbsp oil

200g Bolster Moor home-cured unsmoked thick-cut bacon, diced

2 garlic cloves, finely chopped

400g shallots (or 1 large onion, chopped into large chunks)

250g mushrooms, chopped

300ml beef stock

½ bottle red wine

2 tsp horseradish

Handful of fresh thyme, chopped

Handful of fresh parsley, chopped

375g frozen puff pastry, thawed

Milk, for brushing

Salt and black pepper

Method

Toss the meat in some seasoned flour so that it's lightly coated. Heat 4 tablespoons of the oil in a large heavy-based pan and add the steak to brown off. You may need to do this in batches. Remove the meat from the pan and set aside, leaving the juices in the pan.

Fry the bacon in the pan until crispy, then remove from the pan and set aside on a plate.

Add another tablespoon of oil to the pan and sauté the garlic and shallots until the shallots are browned. As before, remove them from the pan and set aside on a plate. Repeat with the mushrooms.

Add everything back to the pan with the stock, wine, horseradish and herbs. Season with salt and black pepper and give everything a good stir. Simmer on a low heat for 1½-2 hours or until the meat is tender. Be ready to top up with a little boiling water if you see the liquid levels reducing too much; it should be loose and casserole-like, not too gloopy.

Preheat the oven to 200°c/Gas 6. Transfer the casserole into a big pie dish. Roll out the pastry and cut a circle just bigger than the dish. Mould the extra pastry onto the edge of the pie dish and brush with milk. Put the pastry lid on top and pat down the edges. Make two slits in the top of the pastry and brush with milk. Cook in the oven for 25-30 minutes.

This is lovely served with some green vegetables and a glass of red wine. Enjoy!

Baking the old-fashioned WAY

Back in 1984, Steve Taylor had one issue on his mind: no matter how hard he looked he couldn't find good, real bread anywhere. So he decided to bake it himself! Fast forward to 2016, and Bondgate Bakery have expanded their original premises and now supply some of Yorkshire's finest establishments.

Everything Bondgate Bakery sell is made on-site, from scratch. From their traditional bread and Yorkshire curd tarts, brownies and parkin to quiches and hummus, there are no additives, preservatives or factory-made mixes in anything. Sally, Steve's wife, explains: "It's really important to us that our raw ingredients are pure and unadulterated. That has been our motto since we first started in 1984 and it will never change."

The small market town of Otley welcomed Bondgate Bakery into the community thirty two years ago and Sally could not be more grateful: "Otley has a mix of people from all walks of life and our shop took off straight away, the people really welcomed us. In turn, we try to cater for everyone here, with a wide range of products including numerous gluten-free breads and also healthier bakes such as low sugar cakes. We've built up strong links with our local suppliers and this fuels the community spirit here! It feels good to work together with other local businesses."

Bondgate now employ five bakers and their shop and wholesale business has expanded year on year, but their classic curd tarts are still made according to Steve's grandmother's recipe and so is their flapjack. Traditional bakes made

excellently, you can be sure whatever you purchase from this bakery is made with love. Of course, their traditionally baked bread is the bestseller. Breadmaking is an ancient art, one which the team at Bondgate have spent years perfecting. From wholemeal and seeded varieties to rye and sourdough, Steve and his bakers spend hours every day making each loaf. The slow fermentation process means nutrients and flavour are locked in for that comforting, home-baked taste every time.

With all the right ingredients for success, it comes as no surprise that Bondgate Bakery have been recognised with awards both locally and nationally. Winning 'Best Small Retailer' at the BBC Food and Farming Awards brought the bakery lots of publicity and this year they won 'Best Bakery in the UK' in the Farm Shop and Deli Awards. Sally is really proud: "It's really so rewarding to be recognised on a national scale by our industry peers." Bondgate Bakery have also won 'Best Large Business' in the Otley Business Awards and were finalists in the Yorkshire Post Taste Awards last year. With accolades rolling in from locals and industry professionals alike, it's clear that this bakery will continue to build on its already well-established reputation, with a long and bright future ahead.

Bondgate Bakery
CHERRY AND WHITE CHOCOLATE BROWNIE

These cherry and white chocolate brownies are the perfect teatime treat. You can substitute the cherries and white chocolate for any filling you fancy!

Preparation time: 15 minutes | Cooking time: 35 minutes | Makes 12 brownies

Ingredients

350g good quality dark chocolate

300g butter

200g dark muscavado sugar

3 free-range eggs

125g white wheat flour

1 tsp baking powder

100g glace cherries, chopped in half

100g white chocolate chunks

Method

Line a 18x18cm tin with baking parchment and preheat the oven to 190°c.

Melt the dark chocolate and the butter together in a saucepan on a medium heat, stirring constantly.

Once the butter and chocolate are melted and combined, remove the pan from the heat and pour the mixture into a large mixing bowl with the muscavado sugar. Mix this together well.

Whisk in the eggs and fold in the flour and baking powder.

Once the mixture is fully combined, pour it into the lined tray and sprinkle over the cherries and white chocolate chunks.

Bake in the oven for 35 minutes or until the brownies are formed but still soft to the touch.

Follow the NORTH STAR

For the last twelve years this iconic Yorkshire restaurant has retained a Michelin star, three AA rosettes and more than a few esteemed recommendations in some of the country's best food guides; keeping Ilkley on Yorkshire's culinary map since it first opened in the 60s.

The building itself is one of the oldest in Ilkley. Originally a stone farmhouse dating back to 1720, it was once home to a generation of gentleman farmers. It was in the late nineteenth century that box trees were first planted in the front garden and accordingly the property became known as Box Tree cottage.

First opening as a fine dining restaurant in 1962, The Box Tree soon became recognised as a heavyweight in the industry, gaining two Michelin stars by the early 70s and hence becoming a training ground for some of Britain's finest chefs. Since 2004 The Box Tree has been in the very capable hands of husband and wife team Simon and Rena Gueller, who are more than succeeding in upholding and adding to its reputation for exceptional dining. Chef proprietor Simon, who has personally held a Michelin star for some seventeen years, has worked with and taught some of the UK's best chefs.

Having always admired great French chefs and the French approach to cooking in particular, the style of cooking at The Box Tree is modern but it never strays far from its classical roots, with an emphasis on using the finest ingredients and local produce. The menu changes regularly depending on seasonal availability but you can expect delights such as scallops with celeriac pureé, fillet of Yorkshire beef with wild mushrooms, daube en cassolette and potato foam or fillet of turbot with purple broccoli and brown shrimps and almond.

Each dish that leaves the kitchen showcases both Simon and head chef Mark Owen's dedication to fine food. Alongside fine dining comes fine wine and The Box Tree has always been known for its hugely extensive wine list. With a dedicated sommelier and a varied stock to match any and every dish, wine lovers are truly spoilt for choice here.

Of course, dining at The Box Tree is about more than just the food. The plush, yet welcoming antique-furnished lounge and the luxurious dining rooms combine history and good taste with high quality modern dining. The old school restaurant formality that The Box Tree used to be known for has been replaced with a warm welcome and a comfortable and relaxed approach, yet retaining all the professional style and service one would expect at this level. The front of house team, led by general manager Andrew Pratt, is dedicated to delivering first class customer service. Andrew began his career as a commis waiter at The Box Tree in 1988 and has worked for most of his 29 year career in some of the North's finest restaurants. Rena explains: "We're a team here at The Box Tree and right from the moment a guest is welcomed in the door to the moment they leave, all that matters to us is ensuring that the time they spend here is a memorable dining experience."

It is this attitude that has enabled Simon, Rena and the whole team to restore and retain The Box Tree's iconic status.

THIS BUILDING
WAS OFFICIALLY OPENED
BY
SHIRLEY BASSEY
DECEMBER 5TH. 1971

BOX TREE
RESTAURANT
ESTᴰ. 1962

The Box Tree

HAND-DIVED SCALLOPS WITH BUTTERNUT SQUASH, PARMESAN AND PEDRO XIMENEZ JELLY

This dish may look complex but it's sure to wow any dinner party guest.

Preparation time: 2 hours | Cooking time: 15 minutes | Serves 1

Ingredients

For the jelly:
100ml Pedro Ximenez sherry
1 pinch salt
1 tsp caster sugar
1 tsp vege-gel

For the Parmesan purée:
150g potatoes, peeled and diced
150g Parmesan
150g crème fraîche

For the butternut squash purée:
1 butternut squash
1 pinch salt
175g butter

For the Parmesan foam:
150ml water
1 pinch salt
50g Parmesan
5g lecithin

For the pickled butternut squash:
1 butternut squash
150ml white wine
150ml white wine vinegar
150g caster sugar
1 star anise

For the scallops:
2 large hand-dived fresh scallops
50g butter
1 tbsp lemon juice
Olive oil

For the garnish:
1 tbsp Parmesan puff
1 tbsp pumpkin seeds, toasted
Rocket cress, to sprinkle on top
1 tbsp Parmesan powder

Method

For the jelly

Place all of the ingredients in a saucepan and bring to the boil. Once the mixture is boiling, remove from the heat. Pass the mix through a fine sieve and leave to set in the fridge.

For the Parmesan purée

Vacuum pack the chopped and diced potatoes and cook at 85°c for an hour and a half.

Once the potatoes are cooked, blend them in a food processor with the Parmesan and crème fraîche until a smooth consistency is achieved. Pass the mixture through a fine sieve and spoon into a piping bag to use when assembling the dish.

For the butternut squash purée

Peel, deseed and dice the butternut squash. Heat the butter in a large saucepan on a medium heat, add the butternut squash and season with salt to taste. Cover the pan and sweat the squash for 20 minutes. Once the squash is cooked and soft, blend it using a food processor and again pass this mixture through a sieve.

For the Parmesan foam

Place all of the ingredients in a saucepan and bring it to the boil. Once boiling, remove the pan from the heat. Pass the Parmesan mixture through a sieve.

For the pickled butternut squash

Pass the butternut squash through a spiralizer to make squash spaghetti. Add the white wine, white wine vinegar, caster sugar and star anise to a saucepan and bring to the boil. Once the pickling liquid is boiling, remove it from the heat and pour over the squash. Set aside to cool and pickle.

For the scallops

Heat the oil in a frying pan until hot. Season the scallops with salt and then place into the hot pan. Cook the scallops for 30 seconds on each side, add butter and lemon juice and cook for a further 30 seconds on each side until they develop a golden brown colour.

Take the scallops out of the pan and leave them to rest for 2 minutes before plating.

To serve

Smear the butternut squash purée on the base of the plate then dress the dish as shown in the photograph, using your own creativity with all the other elements.

Chef's tip: don't plate the foam until the last minute before serving.

It's easy being GREEN

After working in an entirely different industry for over a decade, Kat Brown (now Collington) decided to shake things up when an opportunity arose to open her own café in the West Yorkshire village of Rawdon.

Kat's background in marketing for an architectural firm hasn't gone without its merits; inspiration from food retail clients and experience of good design has ensured Brown's Greens looks the part. Working with her business partner and husband, Nick on the design and layout for the café, they capitalised on the vast windows, focused on crisp white walls and reclaimed timber throughout, creating a Scandi-inspired interior. Fresh flowers finish each table and a friendly team makes for a modern and welcoming atmosphere. This combined with a love of all things food, home making, friends and a desire to work for herself meant it wasn't long until Kat realised her dream.

In just one year, with the support of Morgan and Kirsty, integral members of the team since the café opened, Brown's Greens has become something of a community hub. The one-off themed menus and quiz nights complement the daily array of exciting vegetarian dishes and cakes on offer. The menu created by Kat herself, centres around dishes that are simple, healthy and full of flavour. Breakfast includes everything from eggy bread to avocado with halloumi, and their breakfast bowls piled high with scrambled eggs, roast tomatoes, mushrooms and beans offer a hearty start to the day. For lunch, varieties of mini filo pies, daily curries, soups, stews and salads are the menu's staples, while there's the Tasting Delights platter for those customers who just can't decide, offering a little bit of everything from the delightful array of salads from the deli fridge.

A community effort, the café's cakes are baked by Crescent Bakery, raw food treats by Happi Food, mouth watering samosas by Kachumber Kitchen and bread is from French bakery Croissant d'Or, just up the road. The same quality control applies to the beverages; coffee is provided by local roasters North Star and their selection of teas are from Birdhouse Tea Company. Add milk from organic farm Acorn Dairy and you begin to see the map of suppliers that Kat has carved out for the company.

While the vegetarian aspect of the business was always a key requirement for Kat, she decided not to market it too heavily, in the knowledge it may put some meat-eaters off: "It's all about bags of flavour, and healthy wholesome options that offer an alternative to your standard sandwich and jacket potato fare. While we also offer vegan and gluten-free options, a good majority of our customers don't actually have any specific dietary requirements, and simply enjoy the fact that we have healthier, alternative options to a traditional café menu. It's all very accessible; there are curries, salads and exciting dishes full of flavour, as well as hearty classics like cheese and beans on toast."

If people come for the food, they return time and time again for the service. A space to relax, the tables are purposefully not too cramped together, while regulars are greeted with their favourite drinks and dishes, and families with young children are looked after with books, toys and games. If early customer feedback is anything to go by, it looks like Brown's Greens will be a firm favourite on Rawdon's high street for many years to come.

BROWN'S GREENS

Brown's Greens
FLAPJACK BITES

These healthy alternative flapjack balls are delicious and so easy to make. Great for the little ones' lunch boxes, for busy folk to keep hunger at bay at work, or simply as a nice but not naughty treat with a cuppa tea.

Preparation time: 2.5 hours | Cooking time: 20 minutes | Makes 12 large, or 24 small bites

Ingredients

270g good quality peanut butter

340g honey

250g oats

For the topping:

40g pistachios, chopped

75g white chocolate

Rose Petals (optional)

Method

In a non-stick pan, over a low heat melt the peanut butter and honey together, so the two ingredients combine and become thinner in consistency.

Turn off the heat and add the oats. Mix with a wooden spoon. The mixture should start to combine, but not all come together – it should be clumpy.

Empty the contents of the pan on a tray, spread out evenly and place in the fridge to cool.

Remove the pistachios from their shells and roughly chop.

After about 1 hour, remove the flapjack mix from the fridge. At this point start to melt the chocolate in a heatproof bowl, over simmering water (this is called a ban-marie method). Keep the chocolate to one side once melted.

Divide the mixture up into equal portions and roll into balls with your hands. You can either make about 12 large flapjack balls or 24 small balls.

Drizzle the chocolate over using a teaspoon and sprinkle over the toppings.

Place on tray and refrigerate for a further 30-60 minutes to allow the chocolate to set.

Enjoy!

Spicing up the
VEGETABLES

There's no better moniker to represent the collaboration of two of West Yorkshire's thriving food and drink hotspots; Prashad and The Sparrow. Originating from Urdu, and derived from the Persian term 'band-o-bast' meaning 'tying and binding', these differing operations have weaved their areas of expertise together to create something simple yet spectacular.

While the concept of washing a curry down with a beer isn't a wholly revolutionary pairing, Bundobust have taken things one step further, offering a vast yet carefully considered selection of craft beer and real ale, to be paired with a menu of 15 Gujarat-inspired vegetarian street food dishes.

It all started when Mark Husak of The Sparrow craft beer café in Bradford teamed up with Mayur Patel from popular Indian restaurant Prashad for a one-off food and drink pairing evening. Following a few more sold-out events, the pair took to the road with a pop-up restaurant, allowing them to test recipes, scope out what worked and refine their process.

After an overwhelmingly good response, in 2014 they made it permanent, and opened up shop on Mill Hill in Leeds city centre. Since then their laid-back approach has welcomed thousands through the doors, whether it's for a taste of their popular okra fries and biryani bhaji balls (the fiery bigger brother of Italian arancini), or to sample their ever-changing selection of craft beer.

"It's a more exciting approach to vegetarian food, and that's what people are after. There's definitely a growing trend towards eating less meat these days – the majority of our customers aren't vegetarians, but choose to go meat-free for at least a couple of days a week. And that's where we come in, offering a more interesting approach," explains owner Mark Husak.

Their regular menu is complemented by seasonal specials that often involve some kind of cultural crossover; think Gobi kofta and currywurst sauce or sauerkraut fritters for Oktoberfest, and sprout bhajis for the festive season.

On top of being animal-friendly, Bundobust are environmentally conscious too. Their plates and pots are one hundred percent biodegradable, and their cutlery is made from plant starch, so completely compostable.

With a listing in the Michelin guide and a second venue opening in Manchester, the Bundobust team are only just getting things started.

Bundobust
ONION GOBI BHAJI

This variation on the traditional bhaji is a firm favourite at Bundobust, combining onion, cauliflower and spinach.

Preparation time: 25 minutes | Cooking time: 10 minutes | Makes 12 bhajis

Ingredients

2 onions

1 small cauliflower

1 bunch spinach

1 tbsp whole coriander seeds

1 tsp ajwain seeds

1 red chilli, crushed

2 medium green chillies, chopped

1 tsp salt

125g gram flour

Sunflower oil, for deep frying

Handful coriander, chopped

Method

Finely chop the onion, cauliflower and spinach.

Mix together all of the spices (coriander seeds, ajwain, crushed red chilli, green chillies and salt). Once mixed add all fresh ingredients and squeeze the dry ingredients through the fresh vegetables, encouraging the natural moisture to be released.

Cover and set aside for 15-20 minutes.

Add the gram flour and mix through once more ensuring all the spices and gram flour are combined to form a batter. Form the mixture into 12 small balls and set aside. Heat some oil (enough to deep fry the bhajis) to 160°c. The bhajis will be quite loose in consistency but don't worry. Reform the shape and gently lower into the oil. If you would prefer this can be done with a spoon but this may not give you the perfect shape.

Fry until golden brown and drain on some kitchen paper. Serve piping hot with some yoghurt raita, chopped coriander and salad.

Appsolutely ITALIAN

Buon Apps have been providing the people of Otley with an authentic taste of Italy since 2003. The team look forward to welcoming you.

The Family

Born into a family of restaurateurs in Rome, food has always been a big part of Alessandro's life. He began working in his parent's restaurant at an early age, where their passion for people and good food became ingrained in him too, eventually leading to the opening of Buon Apps with his wife Elena Sofia in 2003. Elena Sofia grew up in Leicestershire where her Italian father cooked traditional dishes reminiscent of his childhood in Rome. Spending long family holidays in Italy introduced her to the delights of Italian cuisine, culture and service, something she has carried forward into the business.

The Food

Buon Apps serves authentic and traditional Italian food inspired by the great regions of Italy. Using recipes passed down the generations, and some well-guarded family secrets, Alessandro and Elena Sofia simply want their food to be the best Italian food you've ever tasted. Raw passion, and a desire to give every guest an exceptional experience is what drives them and it is their attention to detail that sets Buon Apps apart. Everything is made on site by head-chef Massimo and his team of six using the finest Yorkshire ingredients and produce sourced directly from Italy. The menu is seasonal, driven by what's at its best and freshest. Expect to find a wide selection of pastas, stone-baked pizzas and an extensive a-la-carte menu offering dishes familiar to any Italian. All to be enjoyed with authentic Italian beers, wines and spirits!

Every Wednesday the chefs prepare a special three course menu offering flavours from a different Italian region. It's a great way to enjoy dishes not often found outside Italy. Taste and authenticity are incredibly important to the team at Buon Apps, as Alessandro explains: "In Italy, different pastas are created in different regions, to be paired with different foods and sauces, and that is exactly what we do here. We're making real Italian food as you'd find it in Italy."

The Restaurant

At Buon Apps, Yorkshire's industrial heritage and the taste of Italy blend effortlessly. The restaurant is set in a converted 1870s spinning mill in a beautiful setting by the River Wharfe. Weather permitting, guests can enjoy a drink by the river, soaking up the view. Exposed brickwork and dark wood fittings give the restaurant a distinctly intimate, romantic feel; the perfect place to enjoy a candlelit dinner for two or to share good times and great food with friends or family.

We love meeting new guests so be assured you'll receive a warm Italian welcome, authentic cuisine, discreet attentive service and a dining experience to remember!

Buon Apps of Otley
PORCHETTA ALLA TOSCANA

This classic Italian dish of rolled pork belly is filled with the intense flavours of garlic and lemon. Get ready for some excellent crackling!

Preparation time: 20 minutes | Cooking time: 3 hours | Serves 6

Ingredients

For the porchetta:

3kg belly pork joint

3 tbsp rock salt

Olive oil

7 garlic cloves, chopped

1 bunch rosemary, chopped

1 small handful sage, chopped

A few sprigs thyme, chopped

Cracked black pepper, to season

1 lemon, zested

1 full pork fillet

1 litre stock

Butchers string, to tie the pork fillet and belly pork

For the jus:

Flour, to thicken jus

50g unsalted butter

Method

For the porchetta

Score the belly pork joint all over.

Massage some of the rock salt into the skin of the pork belly with a little olive oil.

Mix together the chopped garlic, herbs, rock salt, pepper and lemon zest. Cut the belly pork joint open to flatten it and spread the garlic and herb mixture across the inside.

Cut the pork fillet in half lengthways.

Place the pork fillet in the middle of the cut open and seasoned belly pork joint. Roll the up the pork lengthways and tie together with the butchers string.

Place the porchetta in a deep roasting tin and pour over the stock.

Cover the porchetta with foil and cook in the oven at 170°c for 2 hours. After 2 hours, remove the foil from the porchetta and cook uncovered for a final 30 minutes.

For the jus

Skim and remove the excess fat from the roasting tin and pour the leftover meat juices and stock into a saucepan. Warm on a low heat and add the butter and flour to thicken.

Buon Apps of Otley
CACCIUCCO ALLA LIVORNESE

Cacciucco is a popular traditional seafood dish with a history that stretches back at least five hundred years. This fish stew was first made in Livorno around the year 1500. After having sold what they fished, fishermen's families had to cook with whatever remained unsold, thus starting the tradition of mixing all kinds of fish together.

Preparation time: 15 minutes | Cooking time: 2 hours | Serves 4

Ingredients

250g fresh calamari

250g octopus

1 garlic clove

2 red chillies, chopped

200ml dry white wine

150g cherry tomatoes

600g plum tomatoes, tinned

1kg fresh mussels

8 king prawns, peeled and ready to cook

8 langoustines, shelled and ready to cook

400g white fish, filleted and roughly chopped

1 loaf bread

Parsley, to garnish

Olive oil, to garnish

Black pepper, to garnish

Method

Wash, clean and roughly chop the calamari and octopus.

Place in a pan with the garlic and chopped chillies. Fry the calamari and octopus for about 3 minutes, and then add the white wine. Keep on the heat and let the wine evaporate before adding the cherry and plum tomatoes.

Cover the pan with a lid and gently cook this mixture on a low heat for an hour and a half.

Then add the mussels, prawns, langoustines and the white fish. Replace the lid and cook for a further 5 minutes.

To serve

Slice and toast the Italian bread of choice.

Serve a generous portion of the cacciucco in a bowl with a sprinkle of parsley, a drizzle of olive oil and a pinch of black pepper. Top with the toasted Italian bread and enjoy!

Buon Apps of Otley
BUDINO DI PANETTONE

A sweet and festive alternative to traditional bread pudding, this panettone pudding is incredibly easy to make if you use shop bought panettone. If you're an avid baker, have a go at making your own panettone and use any leftovers to make this tasty dessert.

Preparation time: 10 minutes | Cooking time: 20 minutes | Serves 4

Ingredients

For the custard:

4 eggs, yolks only

125g caster sugar

500ml whipping cream

1 lemon, zest

1 orange, zest

1 cinnamon stick

1 pod vanilla

30ml Grand Marnier

For the bread:

500g Italian panettone

125g butter

Icing sugar, for dusting

Method

Whisk the egg yolks and sugar together in a large mixing bowl for approximately 2 minutes.

To make the custard, place the cream in a saucepan with the lemon and orange zest, cinnamon stick, vanilla pod and Grand Marnier. Heat this mixture on a medium heat until simmering.

Once simmering, remove from the heat and sieve the custard mix. Slowly add it to the whisked eggs and sugar.

Slice the panettone and butter each slice then layer up in a deep tray or ovenproof dish, create preferably two layers. Pour over the mixture and bake in the oven at 145°c for 20 minutes.

To serve

Dust it with icing sugar and serve with more cream!

Foreign recipes, local PRODUCE

The finest North African & Middle Eastern street food made from scratch for those who love good food and authentic flavours.

Step into the hustle and bustle of Kirkgate Market and follow the smells of warm rich spices lingering in the air and you'll stumble across Café Moor which could easily be mistaken for a Moroccan Souk. Founder Kada Bendaha and his other half Nour have been serving up something special since 2013; he has even taken his worldly dishes out on the road and fed many hungry bellies at festivals across the UK.

Born and raised in Algeria, Kada spent many years in France in a quest to nurture his passion for cooking before moving to Leeds to follow his culinary dream. Falafels, hummus, Moroccan mint tea, tagines and chicken shawarmas are just a few of the favourites at Café Moor; think tender chargrilled meat, lashings of homemade harissa sauce, zingy Algerian and Palestinian salad, crunchy pickles and the warming flavours of tahini and baba ganoush – the fragrant Palestinian and North African spices will instantly transport you halfway across the world.

While some people see kebabs as greasy fast food you'd buy on your way home from a night out, Kada has made it his mission to change this concept and reclaim the recipe to its rightful origin. "I want to reintroduce chicken shawarma to everyone and show how it originally came about, how it should taste and how healthy it can be," says Kada. The chicken is soaked in a marinade of fresh yoghurt and Middle Eastern spices overnight to enhance the flavours and bring out the real taste of the meat instead of overpowering it.

All ingredients are bought freshly from Kirkgate Market itself and Kada is a big supporter of local produce and businesses. "Our duty is to keep the market alive and influence more chefs to cook like this, we need to redirect the younger generation to use fresh produce and support the local markets," he says. Numerous awards later, he moved onto a new venture Caravanserai. The English word Caravanserai is loosely translated from the Turkish word Kervansaray, which means "caravan-palace." For many centuries, Caravanserais have been a place for people to meet and eat together, enjoying good food and each other's company.

Caravanserai has the same charm as Café Moor but with the bonus of an upstairs dining area. Intricately patterned Persian rugs festoon the room and Turkish lanterns and shiny Algerian ornaments hang off the walls – the place is fit for an Ottoman prince but the bill will tell you a different story.

Value exceeds price by far at both Café Moor and Caravanserai which means it's healthy, delicious and cheap – too good to be true? Go see for yourself.

Photo: Tom O'D

Café Moor
FESTIVE CHICKEN BASTILLA

Traditionally, this famous Moroccan pie is made with squab pigeon, which are young pigeons specially bred for the table. Chicken is a popular substitute in this dish, even in Morocco. To save time, you can prepare the mixture two days in advance.

Preparation time: 25 minutes | Cooking time: 2 hours 15 minutes | Serves 10

Ingredients

150g butter

1.5kg chicken, quartered or 3 x 500g squab pigeons, halved

2 large red onions, finely chopped

3 garlic cloves, crushed

1 cinnamon stick

1 tsp ground ginger

1 ½ tsp ground cumin

1 ½ tsp cayenne pepper

1 ½ tsp ground turmeric

Pinch of saffron threads soaked in 2 tbsp warm water

500ml chicken stock

1 tbsp lemon juice

3 tbsp parsley, chopped

3 tbsp coriander, chopped

5 eggs, lightly beaten

14 sheets of filo pastry

100g blanched almonds, toasted and finely chopped

3 tbsp icing sugar, plus extra to serve

1 tsp ground cinnamon, plus extra to serve

100g butter, melted

Method

Preheat oven to 160°c.

Melt the butter in a flameproof casserole dish over a medium heat. Brown the chicken or squab well, then set aside.

Add the onion to the dish and cook for ten minutes, or until golden. Stir in the garlic and spices, then the saffron, its soaking liquid and the stock. Add the chicken back in and turn to coat.

Cover and bake, turning occasionally for 1 hour, or until cooked through. Add a little extra water if needed.

Remove the chicken, reserving the sauce. Discard the cinnamon stick and remove the chicken from the bones and cut into small pieces.

Put the sauce, lemon juice and herbs in a saucepan and reduce over a high heat for ten minutes, or until thick. Reduce the heat to very low, gradually stir in the eggs until scrambled, and then remove from the heat. Add the chicken, and season to taste.

Grease a 30cm pizza pan or pie plate with the melted butter and increase the oven temperature to 180°c.

Mix the almonds with the icing sugar and cinnamon and stack eight sheets of filo pastry and brush the top sheet with butter. Place that sheet evenly across the pan with the ends overhanging. Repeat with the next seven sheets, brushing and fanning sheets to cover the pan, with the pastry overhanging evenly all around.

Fill with the chicken mixture and smooth over. Fold four of the flaps back over, then brush with butter and sprinkle with the almond mixture. Fold the other four sheets over and brush the top with butter. Brush the remaining six filo sheets with butter, fanning onto the pie as before.

Using kitchen scissors, cut the excess pastry evenly around the edge about 3cm from the edge of the pan. Using a spatula to lift up the edge of the pie, tuck the overhanging pastry underneath.

Bake for 45-50 minutes, or until golden. Sift icing sugar and cinnamon on top to serve.

Café Moor
HONEY BAKLAVA

We don't really do dessert in the Middle East. We do tea - tea and Baklava. The origins of Baklava are not well documented and many countries have their own version of this syrup-soaked treat. Greeks like using walnuts in theirs, Arabs use cashews and Turks predominantly use pistachios. Some add spices and some don't. In my version, I like to add a little zesty citrus kick to cut through the sweetness. We always serve Baklava with Moroccan mint tea to settle the stomach and delight the palate.

Preparation time: 20 minutes | Cooking time: 1 hour | Serves 8-10

Ingredients

For the pastry:

300g ground almonds

100g pistachio nut slivers or blanched pistachio nuts

100g caster sugar

Rind of 2 oranges, finely grated

Rind of 1 lime, finely grated

6 green cardamom pods, seeds only ground with a pestle and mortar

Pinch of ground cinnamon

150g unsalted butter, melted

2 packets of filo pastry (12 sheets)

For the syrup:

200ml water

1 tbsp lemon juice

50ml honey

1 tsp orange blossom water or rose water

300g caster sugar

Method

For the pastry

Preheat the oven to 180°c or fan 160°c.

Combine the ground almonds, pistachios, caster sugar, and orange and lime rind in a mixing bowl with the ground cardamom seeds and cinnamon.

Grab a 25-30cm square ovenproof dish and brush the base well with melted butter. Line the base of the dish with 6 sheets of filo pastry - ensure there are enough of the sheets overhanging the edge of the dish to allow you to fold them over the contents of the dish later, when it comes to sealing to baklava.

Brush the exposed base of the pastry generously with melted butter, then add the nut mixture into the base and flatten it gently to lightly compress the mixture.

Use five of the remaining six sheets of filo pastry to top the nut mixture as evenly and neatly as possible, then tuck in the loose flaps from the bottom layers.

Add the final sheet of pastry on top to seal the baklava and brush the top layer generously with more melted butter.

Using a very sharp knife, carefully cut diagonal lines or squares across the top layers of pastry. Bake for 25-30 minutes, or until the pastry is golden brown

For the syrup

Combine the water, lemon juice, honey and flavouring into a saucepan and set over a low-medium heat. Dissolve the sugar in the mixture and stir occasionally until the liquid begins to thicken to a syrup consistency – this should take 20-25 minutes.

Remove the baklava from the oven and immediately drizzle the syrup over the pastry. Allow it to seep into all the cuts that you made before baking and allow to cool completely in the tin before cutting.

Dining with a VIEW

Located on the fifth and sixth floor of the Trinity Leeds shopping centre, Crafthouse and Angelica are designed to deliver you a dining experience like no other.

Two distinctly different brands live under one roof at the Trinity Leeds shopping centre, one offers modern British cuisine with a focus on quality produce and the other is a grand café by day but a cocktail destination by night. One thing that they both offer is a spectacular panoramic view – wine and dine in their exclusive roof terrace or take in the 360° view of the city whilst sipping a cocktail from the highest bar in Leeds.

Senior general manager Mark Morris has worked hard with executive chef Lee Murdoch to curate a menu that highlights the fact that the best dishes start with the best produce. Many ingredients are sourced from local suppliers such as Yorkshire Lager and Wellocks who supply their vegetables, fresh fruit, dairy and cheese. However, their belief in quality pervades everything they do which can sometimes mean looking a little further out – The Orkney Islands is where they get their beef, smoked meats and fish comes from Staal Smokehouse based in East Yorkshire.

"We use special ingredients to cook things you might not be able to do at home – I like to have a story behind what we use and why we use it, it's good for people to learn this for the next generation. I would like more education on game, people tend to shy away from it because it's unusual but when cooked properly it's exquisite!" says Lee.

The menus change with the seasons but at whatever time of the year, you'll find dishes cooked to perfection on their Josper Grill which chargrills their meat, fish and crustaceans at 480°c over charcoal, giving a unique flavour. Upstairs you'll find a tantalising and tempting array of internationally inspired dishes and there's a big push on seafood too – expect oysters, langoustines, hand dived scallops and other great catches of the day.

Internationally renowned DJs regularly visit the penthouse venue – which you can enjoy in stylish surroundings paired with your choice of tipple. Choose from Champagnes, locally sourced beers, wines and an extensive array of classic and signature cocktails, all prepared by a team of skilled mixologists.

Award-winning Crafthouse and Angelica belong to the D&D London group who operate 35 luxury restaurants, bars and hotels across London, New York, Japan and Paris. The huge success of their first venture outside of London in the UK has lead them to open two more new restaurants in Leeds and Manchester next year – exciting times are ahead for the North!

Crafthouse and Angelica
ROAST WOODLAND PIGEON

Roast woodland pigeon with black salsify, foie gras, pigeon faggot and autumn truffle crisp.

Preparation time: 45 minutes | Cooking time: 40 minutes | Serves 4

Ingredients

- 2 woodland pigeons, whole
- Salt and pepper
- 150ml olive oil
- 1 large shallot
- 200g butter
- A few thyme flowers
- Handful of chives, chopped
- 150g foie gras
- 15g fresh truffle
- 500g baby spinach leaves
- 2 chicken breasts
- 400ml double cream
- 1 egg
- 100g pistachios, chopped
- Brioche loaf
- 2 sheets feuille de brick pastry
- 100g crepinette
- 2 large black salsify
- Bowl of lemon water
- Splash of white wine or Pernod
- 2 garlic cloves
- 1 bay leaf
- 150ml cassis
- 250ml chicken jus
- Splash of sherry vinegar
- Handful of brambles
- 1 sprig of thyme
- Nasturtium leaves
- Wild sorrel

Method

For the pigeon, first remove the breast and legs from the bird and remove the skin from the breast and fillet, keep the fillets for the faggot. Season the breast and sear in hot pan with olive oil for 90 seconds on each side then remove and chill in fridge.

For the faggot, remove the skin from the pigeon legs and mince finely with the remaining fillets. Dice the shallot and sweat in a little butter with a few thyme flowers, then leave to cool in the fridge. Mix the cooked shallots with the chopped chives, 50g of the grated foie gras and a teaspoon of chopped truffle. Season to taste and sit aside in the fridge.

Pick 100g of spinach leaves and steam for 50 seconds, chill directly in ice water. Dry off then place 15-25g pieces of the mince mix to a square sheet of spinach, roll in cling film until you have a tight sausage shape then tie each end so it is all sealed.

For the chicken mousse, dice chicken breast and blend in a food processor. Add half the double cream and egg and mix until smooth, this should take around 1-2 minutes. Add seasoning, a teaspoon of finely chopped truffle, chopped pistachios and 100g of spinach, before blending for a further minute. Place in piping bag for later.

For the foie gras crunch, cut foie gras into ½cm width and 2cm length rectangles. Then cut the brioche into around six slices about ½cm thick and 12cm long.

Spread a thin layer of the chicken mousse along the bread then add the foie gras rectangles, roll this in cling film until you have a sausage shape. Tie and place in the fridge for later.

For the truffle crisp, preheat the oven to 180°c and then melt 20g of butter. Lay out the feuille de brick pastry, brush with the melted butter, grate on a teaspoon of truffle and season. Place the other piece of pastry on top and bake for 5-7 minutes.

For the pigeon take the seared pigeon breast from earlier and place 15g pieces of foie gras on top, cover in chicken mousse and use palette knives to smooth off. Apply the crepinette around then leave to set in the fridge for 25 minutes.

For the salsify, peel the black salsify and place in lemon water to stop it going brown. Place the stick in a hot pan with olive oil, allow to colour then add a large knob of butter, when the butter starts to foam, add a splash of white wine or Pernod, a garlic clove and a bay leaf, cook until just soft. Cook in the oven for 25-45 minutes at 180°c until soft.

For the spinach purée, boil the remaining 200ml cream, flame and add seasoning. Add to blender and blend fast adding in 200g of spinach. Add 50g of butter and season.

For the sauce, reduce 150ml of cassis before adding the chicken jus, a splash of sherry vinegar and the brambles, take off the heat and leave to one side. Heat a pan until warm then add some butter, place the pigeon flesh side down and baste the top of mousse with butter for about 45-55 seconds. Add thyme and the other garlic clove and place in the oven for five minutes at 180°c. Allow to rest for 8 minutes. Warm the faggot in the sauce for 3-5 minutes and fry the foie gras crunch in fryer until golden brown.

Assemble with spinach purée on the plate, cut the pigeon in half and arrange the salsify around. Add your woodland forage (nasturtium leaves and wild sorrel) and finish with the sauce and truffle crisp.

The place to meet AND EAT

Nestled in the heart of Chapel Allerton, Crust and Crumb has been serving up tasty food in a friendly and warm environment since 2010.

From a young age Nicola wanted to open a shop selling delicious food, it was just about finding the right opportunity which happened to come along right in the middle of the recession.

Starting out as a simple bakery, Crust and Crumb has evolved into a haven for those seeking out tasty food in a cosy setting. Each day, the counter is filled with all sorts of homemade cakes and treats, from white chocolate and raspberry brownies and salted caramel shortbread to pork and leek sausage rolls, fresh sandwiches and homemade salads. Whether you are hankering for a post yoga nibble or a hangover-curing 'full English', they have got it covered.

Growing up on a North Yorkshire farm Nicola has an inherent appreciation for quality local produce. This is showcased in the range of lovely ingredients used in the kitchen – their meat is from award-winning Lishman's of Ilkley and Sykes House Farm, breads and pastries come fresh from Bondgate Bakery, dressings from Yorkshire Rapeseed Oil, Ian Taylor's for eggs and Bracken Hill supply the jams and chutneys.

Working closely with Jenny the shop manager, they come up with a seasonal and varying menu to cater for all dietary requirements. Summer brings flatbreads and fresh salad bowls, winter is all about toasties and hearty soups – there is always something new to try. The power bar is a year-round favourite; packed with energy-giving goodness to set you up for the day – the recipe for that is a closely guarded secret so instead they've given you the secrets behind a close runners-up, the berry bakewell tart.

People from all walks of life come to socialise at Crust and Crumb whilst admiring their scrumptious array of food, from professionals to pensioners and even dog owners – water dishes and biscuits are provided for well-behaved pooches!

Crust and Crumb is firmly part of the local community. It is the place to grab a quick takeout lunch and also the place to go for barista quality coffee, a wedge of cake and a good natter with friends. There is so much more to be found here that hasn't been mentioned so why not mosey on down and come see for yourself?

CRUST & CRUMB

Artisan Bakery   Delicatessen   Sandwiches   Coff

Crust and Crumb
BERRY BAKEWELL TART

This berry bakewell tart is an all-year-round favourite at our café.
It's delicious, it's wonderfully buttery and I hope you enjoy making it!

Preparation time: 15 minutes | Cooking time: 50 minutes | Serves 4

Ingredients

For the pastry:

150g unsalted butter, diced at room temperature

75g caster sugar

250g plain flour

1 free-range egg

For the filling:

250g ground almonds

250g caster sugar

250g unsalted butter, diced at room temperature

3 free-range eggs

150g strawberry jam

For the topping:

110g fresh raspberries/strawberries

30g flaked almonds

Method

For the pastry

Preheat the oven at 170°c and line and grease a 25cm fluted loose bottom flan case.

Place the butter, sugar and flour in a bowl and use an electric mixer on speed 2 until the mix resembles fine breadcrumbs.

Add the egg and allow the crumb to mix to a paste. (Do not overmix at this stage)

Remove from the mixer and shape the pastry into a ball, leave on the side for 5 minutes.

For the filling

Next combine the ground almonds, caster sugar, butter and eggs together with an electric mixture until light and creamy.

Add a dusting of flour to a flat surface and roll out the pastry with a rolling pin to approximately 5mm thickness.

Carefully place this over your tin and press into the corners making sure all edges are pressed into the tin.

Remove the excess pastry from the top of the tin using a palette knife.

Evenly spread the jam into the base of the tin on top of the pastry using the back of a spoon. Pour the almond filling into the tin and use a spoon to level up the sides.

Evenly place the raspberries and strawberries across the tart into the almond filling, leaving the fruit still visible. Then sprinkle the flaked almonds on top for decoration.

Place in the oven for 50 minutes, after 20 minutes turn the tart around and reduce the oven temperature down to 160°c, baking for a further 30 minutes – the tart should be golden and slightly firm to touch.

Leave to cool down slightly and serve warm with a dollop of fresh cream or a scoop of indulgent ice cream.

The legend-dairy
CHEESEMONGER

Purveyors of cheese and fine foods – Cryer & Stott are a family run cheesemongers based in West Yorkshire with a real passion for local artisan produce.

This family business is headed up by husband and wife team Richard and Clare Holmes, who bought the last Cryer & Stott market stall back in 1998. The market stall sold basic provisions such as milk and cheddar but since then they have grown a reputation for supplying the finest quality Yorkshire produce.

The focus is on sourcing artisan produce from small dairies and farms across the UK and they now supply to over 200 clients including independent retailers, hotels, gastropubs and restaurants. Passionate about what they do, they follow their products from milking parlour to plate and their knowledgeable staff members are trained to know everything there is about each and every product.

Cryer & Stott source over 700 British cheeses as well as a full range of continental goods and you can find these at their retail outlets based in Pontefract, Castleford and Allerton Bywater where their flagship store Samuel Valentine is located. This urban food hall was named after their children and it has a real emphasis on supporting small local producers and their core values of food and family.

Expect artisan bread, handcrafted sausages, cured meats and local ales, you'll also find a bistro style café inside which uses all these delicious ingredients to whip up some real seasonal treats. Don't forget to take your pick of their award-winning cheeses to take home – the Yorkshire Cask, Rhuby Crumble and Duke of Wellington blue cheese are notorious for their robust flavours and are a great accompaniment to many dishes.

The company has become renowned for being specialists in the field and this has given them the opportunity to supply prestigious venues and events. This includes the London 2012 Olympic venues; Harvey Nichols and they once created a seven-tier cheese stack for The British Embassy in Paris which was tasted by The Queen! Grabbing the attention of the Yorkshire folk, this has earnt them the title of Wholesaler Of The Year 2015 at the Deliciously Yorkshire Awards.

The legend-dairy cheesemongers and fine food merchant has built up quite the portfolio over the years, perhaps now you'll consider a tiered cheese stack or pork pie pyramid as an alternative wedding cake – they are sure to be a talking point for years to come!

Cryer & Stott
RHUBY CRUMBLE CHEESECAKE

This cheesecake recipe pays homage to our Yorkshire roots and the famous 'Rhubarb Triangle' which is a stone's throw from our business.
If you've got kids, I encourage you to make this dish with your children as it's quite simple, yet fun!

Preparation time: 25 minutes plus 1½ hours chilling time | Serves 8

Ingredients

200g digestive biscuits, crushed

100g unsalted butter, melted

400g Yorkshire Rhuby Crumble cheese

500g cream cheese

Pouring cream

1 lemon, juiced

Icing sugar to taste

Rhubarb to decorate

Method

First mix together the crushed digestive biscuits and melted butter.

Press the mixture down firmly in an 20cm loose bottomed cake tin to form the base and pop in the fridge for half an hour.

Mix together the Rhuby Crumble cheese and the cream cheese, add enough pouring cream to make the consistency stiff.

Add the juice of one lemon and some icing sugar to taste.

Spread the cheese mixture on top of the biscuit base and refrigerate until it has set - leave it for at least 1 hour.

Before serving decorate the cheese cake with rhubarb and icing sugar!

Interactive EATING

Fazenda takes social dining to a new level with its interactive approach to sharing traditional Brazilian slow-roasted meat in a buzzing, friendly atmosphere.

Nothing represents Fazenda more than beautifully cooked meats and bottles of fine wine being shared amongst friends. But there is also a South American tradition that has been a way of life amongst gaúchos for over a hundred years – and Fazenda is keeping that heritage alive by bringing the unique dining experience to Watermans Place in Leeds.

In the 19th century, gaúchos – or cowboys – travelled across South America herding their cattle. Digging a big pit in the ground, they would slowly cook large pieces of beef over the fire. Gathered around, they would drink wine, tell stories, sing songs and slice off pieces of meat. This social way of eating epitomises the traditions of the gaúchos and the importance that they place on sharing.

Fazenda mirrors this social tradition but with a totally modern take – and the result is something unique. The venue features continuous table-side service of different prime cuts of beef, pork, lamb and chicken, which have been grilled to perfection by gaúcho chefs. Diners are greeted with a warm and friendly welcome, as they begin their Fazenda journey at the bountiful salad bar. Catering for all diners, there is a selection of sushi, cured meats, hot dishes and traditional Brazilian treats – including the classic South-American bean stew, Feijoada.

Guests return to their table and the experience can truly begin. They control the service by flipping their card from red to green which indicates the passadores that the table is ready for one of the freshly grilled cuts of meat. This is when the 'rodizio' (meaning 'to rotate') commences! With continuous tableside service, guests can have a rest in between cuts, request their favourite meats and enjoy the unique experience.

Diners can enjoy freshly grilled joints of meats, served 'churrascaria'-style (straight from the barbecue). When the delicious cuts of meats are prepared, and grilled to perfection, passadores rotate randomly throughout the restaurant offering the guests a taste of Southern Brazil.

Fazenda offers eight cuts of meat at lunchtime and fifteen in the evening, cooked to their own taste. Cuts of beef include picanha (cap of rump) which is their signature cut. It is juicy and full of flavour, melts in the mouth and is very popular with the regular guests.

They also serve the cordeiro, a tender chump of lamb and gently flavoured with fresh mint, or for those of a more experimental nature – coração de frango. A firm favourite at Fazenda amongst the team, the corações de frango (chicken hearts) are an acquired taste but incredibly tender and juicy – a must try!

Frango (grilled chicken thighs basted in a lemon and garlic marinade), barriga de porco (pork belly sliced with a honey, lemon and cinnamon sauce) and linguiça (a Brazilian-style pork and beef sausage, originating from Portugal and famous for its robust flavour) are a few of the other tempting tastes. The meal is also accompanied by some traditional nibbles such as Brazilian cheese breads with chimichurri mayo.

Part of an independent and growing company that also has restaurants in Liverpool and Manchester, Fazenda is not just about the food. With a driven passion for wine, Fazenda showcases a carefully selected wine list; a key ingredient for the restaurants unique experience. From old world to new world styles, inclusive of a comprehensive selection of Argentinian and Brazilian wines, there is an offer for all palates. The wine list unsurprisingly includes bottles from South America's most famous wine regions like Mendoza, Cholchagua and Rapel Valley, including a list of very specially selected gems.

Extensively trained and knowledgeable staff are on hand who can advise on the best wines to accompany your dishes and to suit your preferences. The wine along with the meat and the interactive experience itself all add up to create the deliciously different experience of dining Fazenda-style.

Fazenda
MOQUECA

Moqueca is a traditional fish stew from Salvador du Bahia. We cook a modern version of this dish, but using exactly the same ingredients as the traditional recipe. We thought that the traditional version would be easy to achieve at home as it doesn't include modern cooking techniques.

Preparation time: 15 minutes | Cooking time: 30 minutes | Serves 4

Ingredients

2 tbsp olive oil

200g white onion, roughly diced

350g mixed peppers, roughly diced

2 garlic cloves, roughly diced

250g tomatoes, roughly diced

500g king prawns

500g cod, diced

1 tbsp ground cumin

1 tbsp ground turmeric

1 tsp smoked paprika

1 tsp salt

1 tsp cracked black pepper

800ml coconut milk

Fresh coriander leaves, chopped, to garnish

Method

You can use a wok or paella pan to prepare this recipe.

Heat the olive oil in the wok or paella pan, add the diced onion, peppers, garlic and tomatoes and cook for about 5 minutes. Add the prawns and cod, and continue to cook for 2 minutes more. Add all the spices and seasoning, mix everything well and finally add the coconut milk. Allow to simmer for about 20 minutes, until cooked.

Sprinkle some chopped coriander on top of the stew and serve.

Serve it in the pan on the table to share. Ideally serve it with steamed rice on the side.

Our HOUSE

An independent coffee and tea house in Chapel Allerton serving up an ever changing seasonal menu of locally sourced produce.

Husband and wife team Chris and Shanshan had always talked about starting their own coffee shop, they both came from an IT background but wanted to try something completely different and that's where House of Koko came into play. Thankfully throwing in the towel of the IT world was the right decision as they both dived into the deep end with careless abandon and enthusiastic optimism, resulting in something that they're very proud of.

Retro furnishings, parquet flooring, geometric patterns and exposed brickwork are just a few components of the décor that Shanshan conceptualised through moodboarding and brainstorming ideas with Chris. It's a welcoming and vibrant hub of creativity that caters for all groups, whether you want a place to relax and a chat, get some work done or meet friends with children. "House of Koko is all about good coffee, great food and excellent customer service – we believe that if you focus on those three things, people will keep coming back," says Chris.

The spotlight is on fresh and healthy ingredients at House of Koko, all sourced from local suppliers such as Leeds Bread Co-op, North Star Coffee, George and Joseph Cheesemongers and Tarbett's Fishmongers. Mental health charity Growing Better have also got involved by supplying them with freshly picked salad leaves.

Their eye for detail in their interior is just as apparent in their menu of comforting brunches, in-house bakes and specialist teas, making sure every dish is utterly instagrammable. Favourites such as 'The old boy' have been there since day one – crushed avocado on grilled sourdough with chillies, pine nuts and dressed radish. All cakes and bakes are homemade and they use this as a platform for staff to get creative and come up with their own cake concoctions in the Koko bake off!

For an evening of fine dining, try out one of their pop-up restaurant events. This is where House of Koko give talented chefs an opportunity to flex their creative muscles and cook up some delectable dishes for some very lucky guests. Polish street vendor Smak! once set up a barbecue on their decking to serve up specialist sausages and dumplings to the masses. "We know we don't have all the answers so we're happy to collaborate with other people, it's important that we keep our customers curious," says Chris.

House of Koko

HOUSE OF KOKO

House of Koko

BUTTERNUT SQUASH AND FETA TARTE TATIN

To us fresh seasonal produce is the staple of our menu and this tart is kept simple to allow the quality of the produce shine through. Fresh feta is added on top to cut through the richness of the caramelised squash and buttery pastry. It's a great autumnal dish, a staff favourite and can easily be adapted for winter with beetroot and goats cheese.

Preparation time: 20 minutes | Cooking time: 1 hour | Serves 6

Ingredients

26cm circle of butter puff pastry

1 whole butternut squash

2 garlic cloves

3 sprigs of thyme

Drizzle of rapeseed oil or olive oil

65g caster sugar

100g feta cheese

1 egg

Salt and pepper

50g salted butter

35g roasted hazelnuts

Small handful of red mustard frills

Method

Preheat the oven to 180°c and remove the pastry from the fridge to get to room temperature or it will crack when rolled out.

Peel the butternut squash and slice into thin half moons around 5cm thick.

Finely chop the garlic and in a bowl mix the chopped squash, garlic, thyme and oil together and season with salt and pepper.

In a 26cm non-stick frying pan, slowly melt the sugar until if forms a light brown caramel and remove from the heat. Allow to cool slightly.

Arrange a layer of the squash into the pan on top of the caramel in a nice neat design, as this top layer will be on show when served.

Crumble a quarter of the feta over the squash and then arrange the rest of the squash on top making sure you have an even layer throughout the pan.

Once all the squash is arranged, crumble another quarter of the feta then snuggly fit the pastry on top.

Make sure the pastry fits nicely without any gaps, then egg wash and sprinkle with salt, pepper and some thyme leaves.

Bake in the oven for around 45 minutes until the pastry is crisp and golden brown and has puffed up slightly.

Once removed from the oven place a large plate on top of the pan and carefully flip the pan over so that the tart comes out. Be very careful not to get the hot caramel on yourself.

Melt the butter on a medium heat until slightly brown and add the hazelnuts, heating for about 2-3 minutes to make a beurre noisette.

Crumble on the rest of the feta and drizzle a tablespoon of the buerre noisette over and around the tart. Garnish with the red mustard frills.

Welcome to THE CLUB

Hyde Park Book Club is a gathering place for sharing ideas, creativity and friendliness – but it's also a place to eat good food and drink great drinks...

Started in October 2015, Hyde Park Book Club has had its fair share of local and national media coverage since it opened its doors. A creative space for people who want to chat, watch films and enjoy live music amongst a plethora of other things, it has become home to all sorts of regular and one-off events – talks on progressive politics, creative and professional workshops, DJs playing anything from jazz to reggae, record fairs, poetry performances... the list goes on.

Despite such a variety of events happening, it is the food that has created a huge stir – with mentions not just in local press, but also featuring in national newspapers. The Telegraph were shouting about them within just a few months of opening due to their vegetarian menu. They are currently the only place in the UK stocking the products of Dutch mock meat-maker, Vegetarian Butcher. Their meat-free burgers, sausages and chicken are made with plant protein but look, feel and taste like the real thing.

However, the fact that the menu is veggie isn't something the team particularly make a fuss about. It is almost irrelevant that the food is meat-free – what matters is that it tastes amazing and is available for everyone to enjoy. It gives the feeling of inclusivity that is part of the ethos at Hyde Park Book Club.

"We open at 10am daily, close at 11pm and there's always a chilled vibe, with the second space often providing home to a party, exhibition or gathering of some kind," explains co-founder Jack. As a variety of people are welcomed into the venue throughout the day, the menu reflects this diversity.

Veggie breakfasts are served all day, with breakfast bagels containing Vegetarian Butcher sausages, spinach, egg and avocado being popular alongside simple sausage and egg sandwiches, granola or toast. Vegetarian Butcher specials include the Hyde Park hot dog, Book Club burger and chicken skewers, and there are other sandwiches, wraps and snacks to choose from, too.

Good food needs good tea and coffee, great wine and even better beers and the team have gone out of their way to make sure their menu offers something a cut above the usual. From locally roasted coffee and loose-leaf tea to craft beers and unusual small batch spirits, this local gem is quickly establishing a reputation across the city and beyond.

Hyde Park Book Club

BACON DOUBLE CHEESEBURGER AND ELVIS SHAKE

Once we tried the Veg Butcher vegetarian meat, we had to import it. We think it's the best out there. Follow it with a shake made up of chocolate, peanut butter, honey and banana and you'll be in food heaven! Make it a boozy shake with an optional shot of rum.

Preparation time: Approx. 10 minutes | Cooking time: Approx. 10 minutes | Serves: 1

Ingredients

For the burger:

2 Vegetarian Butcher burger patties

1 small handful Vegetarian Butcher smoky bacon strips

1 brioche burger bun

Mixed leaves

1 slice beefsteak tomato

Red onion, sliced

Pickled gherkin

2 slices mature cheddar

Ketchup, mustard and mayo

Vegetable oil, for cooking

For the Elvis shake:

1 tbsp chocolate spread

1 tbsp good quality peanut butter

1 tbsp honey

1 ripe banana

250ml milk

Shot of rum (optional)

2 ice cubes

Cocoa powder, for dusting

Method

For the burger

Preheat a frying pan or griddle to medium hot. Add a small amount of vegetable oil to the pan and fry both burger patties, turning frequently. After 4 minutes add the bacon strips to the pan.

Meanwhile prepare your bun. Slice in half and lightly toast the brioche bun. Spread mayonnaise on the lower half of the bun, then add a layer of mixed salad leaves. Top with the tomato slice. Put ketchup and mustard on the top half of the bun and scatter over slices of red onion and pickled gherkin to your taste. Put the cheese on top of the burger patties and allow to melt slightly.

Assemble your burger – place both patties on top of each other on the bun, then top with the bacon strips. Pop the top on and secure in place with a small skewer.

For the Elvis shake

Place all the ingredients into a blender and blend thoroughly. Pour into glass and dust lightly with cocoa powder.

Spanish STYLE

A new addition to the cosmopolitan dining scene of Leeds, Ibérica serves traditional and modern Spanish cuisine using the finest ingredients.

A Grade II listed building rich in history, Hepper House has become home to Ibérica and its beautiful deli and wine bar La Bodega. The former auction house has the benefit of high ceilings and large windows, not to mention the incredible lightwell, which gives it a feel of grandeur and luxury in the heart of the city centre.

It is set over two floors with La Bodega in the basement and the restaurant itself set beneath the stunning lightwell on the ground floor. A versatile events space on the first floor (The Hepper Room) completes this beautiful building. The interior has been thoughtfully designed to fit with the building's history, as well as to make sure it is the perfect backdrop to the impressive food on offer.

Iberica's menu has been created by Ibérica's world-renowned executive head chef Nacho Manzano, who currently has an impressive three Michelin stars to his name (two for his highly celebrated Casa Marcial and one for La Salgar). He directs a highly experienced team at Ibérica through group head chef, César García. Manzano is renowned for his speciality fish dishes and his modern interpretations of traditional Spanish cooking. The menu ranges from classic tapas dishes to traditional paella, as well as a full à la carte and sumptuous drinks menu.

Inspirational modern Spanish dishes are created using authentic Spanish produce, reflecting Nacho Manzano's style of cooking. His belief in cuisine based around fine products, traditionally made is at the heart of Ibérica's philosophy. There is a commitment to quality which is highlighted in the relationships that Ibérica has forged with producers across Spain.

The wine list has also been carefully considered to complement all the different types of food – from a glass to enjoy with a selection of small plates to a bottle to pair with a freshly cooked paella. The food is served in the traditional way, so diners can enjoy olives, bread, anchovies, artisan cheeses or cured meats including the famous jamón Ibérico before indulging in traditional or contemporary tapas or main dishes… each one presented on the plate as beautifully as the restaurant in which it is served.

Ibérica
HAM CROQUETAS

Ibérica's version of this famous Spanish classic
is becoming famous across Leeds.

Preparation time: 45 minutes plus overnight for the sauce | Cooking time: 2 minutes | Serves: 6

Ingredients

75g Serrano ham

500ml whole milk

40ml olive oil

50g plain flour

Pinch of salt

Beaten eggs, for coating

Breadcrumbs, for coating

Sunflower oil, for deep frying

Method

For the croquetas mix

Dice the ham. Heat the milk until simmering. Heat the olive oil on a medium heat in a saucepan. Add the ham to the saucepan. Cook until the ham becomes browned. Stir in the flour and mix to a basic roux. Whisk in the hot milk a little at a time, then bring to the boil whisking continuously to prevent lumps. Cook this for about 30-45 minutes and add the salt. Pour the sauce into a container, leave to cool then cover with cling film and chill for 24 hours.

To shape the croquetas

Oil both your palms. Scoop the croquetas mix in to your hands and shape into croquetas. Coat with beaten egg and roll it in the breadcrumbs until fully coated. Repeat until all the mixture has been used up and keep in the fridge for a few hours before frying.

To fry the croquetas

Place sunflower oil in a pan and heat to about 180˚c. Deep fry the croquetas for about 2 minutes or until they are golden brown on all sides. Drain off any extra fat on to an absorbent kitchen paper and serve immediately.

The B's KNEES

Ira B's "just off Street Lane" in a leafy suburb of North Leeds, is the go-to place for a proper comfort food fix, with self-professed "bonkers" staff, an eccentric proprietor and a menu of hearty Jewish dishes.

A Leeds girl born and bred, Ira B. Silverman returned to her home city following culinary training at the world-renowned Tante Marie School of Cookery in Woking, Surrey. Wanting to work for herself, Ira started her catering company in 1986 and has been her own boss ever since. A couple of years ago, a world away from that, she opened her Snack Bar Ira B's. Focusing on the American-Jewish deli concept, the plates are piled high with food that makes you smile.

There's a clear nostalgic element to Ira B's, with much of the menu boasting her grandmother's version of classic Jewish dishes. When Ira was three, her grandmother Lily aka Libky, came to live with the family, after Ira's grandfather passed away. Grandma Libky would share food from her Russian-Jewish heritage. For the Silvermans it wasn't uncommon to have two meals to choose from on an evening, whether it was her mother Davreen's traditional shepherd's pie or her grandmother's chopped liver followed by chicken schnitzel and latkes. Naturally, Ira's interest in food began around this time. She realised at an early age that she had the ability to work out exactly what was in a dish simply by tasting it, a skill that has been fundamental in reviving traditional family recipes and making them her own.

A firm favourite on the menu is the 'chuck soup' with lokshen (fine vermicelli) and knaidlach (dumplings); the old saying of chicken soup as 'Jewish penicillin' couldn't ring more true here! Customers often pop in to take some away for friends or family who are unwell.

A close second is the mighty Grobber, a salt beef sandwich on rye that prides itself on containing "more meat than you can eat." What makes this super-size sarnie special – apart from the sheer size of the thing – is the brisket. Pickled in brine for ten days then slow cooked for four hours, this results in a wonderfully tender texture and unique flavour. Since starting her business in '86 Ira has used the same local family butchers which delivers consistent high quality.

Vintage décor comprising of upcycled furniture, 'tongue in cheek' paraphernalia and plenty of other little eccentric touches (check out their LP-sized menus) means there's nowhere quite like this in Leeds, or indeed, this side of the Atlantic.

Ira B's

YOU KNOW, SOMEBODY ACTUALLY COMPLIMENTED ME ON MY DRIVING TODAY. THEY LEFT A LITTLE NOTE ON THE WINDSCREEN, IT SAID 'PARKING FINE.'

Ira B's
GRANDMA LIBKY'S FAMOUS CHOPPED LIVER AND CHICKEN SCHNITZEL SANDWICH

These two recipes are absolute favourites in our snack bar.

Preparation time: 10 minutes | Cooking time: 20 minutes | Liver serves 4 as a starter or 1 as a sandwich

Ingredients

For the chopped liver:

450g chicken livers

1 large onion

2 tbsp sunflower oil

1 tsp granulated sugar

Salt and white pepper, to taste

5 eggs, hard-boiled

Parsley, to garnish (optional)

For the chicken schnitzel sandwich:

115g plain flour

2 medium sized eggs, beaten

115g Japanese panko breadcrumbs

Salt, white pepper and garlic granules, for seasoning

225g large chicken breast, skinned

2 tbsp mayonnaise

¾ tbsp sweet chilli sauce

1 plain bread roll (or roll of your choice), cut in half

Sunflower oil, for deep frying

Iceberg lettuce, shredded

1 dill pickle, sliced lengthways

Method

For the chopped liver:

Clean the chicken livers, removing only the stringy membranes and discoloured parts.

Peel the onion and chop into large chunks.

Heat the oil in a large frying pan.

Add the onions, sprinkle on the sugar and sauté until transparent and starting to soften.

Add the livers and stir fry until coated and sealed. Season with 1 teaspoon each of salt and white pepper.

Continue to cook on a medium heat until the livers are no longer pink inside. Place aside to cool. When cool slice 4 of the eggs and add to the liver and onion mix.

Transfer the mix to a food processor and blitz until a coarse paste.

Place into a mixing bowl. Check the seasoning, adding more salt and pepper to taste.

Turn out and place on a serving plate or into a mould and decorate with the remaining egg by grating the yolk and white separately.

Finely chop the parsley and sprinkle over to finish.

For the chicken schnitzel sandwich:

Set up the pane station: three shallow bowls, one with seasoned plain flour, one with seasoned egg, one with seasoned crumbs.

Split the chicken breast to make two thin fillets.

Dip each breast into the flour until covered completely, then into egg, and finally into the panko breadcrumbs until covered completely. Press until flattened. Repeat with second fillet and place both aside.

Mix the mayonnaise and sweet chilli until combined. Spread onto the cut roll, reserving a bit for the middle of the sandwich.

Heat the oil in a deep frying pan until hot, 190°c. Fry the coated chicken breasts until golden brown on both sides. This will take around 4-5 minutes.

Remove and drain on kitchen paper. Place one fillet on each side of the bread.

Add the lettuce, sliced pickle and more sauce.

Close together, slice in half and serve.

Treasured MOMENTS

Step back in time at Jameson's Café and Tea Room in Oakwood, where the ritual of tea time is cherished.

Jameson's Café and Tea Rooms began life in Sheffield, where the family name has been known in the city's antique business since 1883. Sarah Jameson had dreamed of opening a traditional tearoom that completely embraced the charms of a bygone era. Sharing a pot of tea with her mother one day, she was delighting in the age-old traditions that come with drinking tea – taking time to sit down and to just let time stop for a while, the ritual of allowing the tea to brew to perfection, the ceremony of pouring it into delicate china cups and the joy of savouring the taste.

Following the success of her first tea room, she was delighted to be able to open a second branch in the leafy area of Oakwood on bustling Roundhay Road. With Roundhay Park on the doorstep, Sarah couldn't think of a more perfect setting for her tranquil tea room.

From walking through the doors, it is like stepping back in time. Customers are greeted with old-fashioned friendliness and warmth that is often overlooked in the rush of modern life. She went to every effort to make sure she achieved tea-time perfection in her café with no aspect of the service,

ambience, food or drink overlooked. Her well-trained staff greet guests with genuine warmth and their attention to detail never falters, meaning that every customer leaves feeling like they have been well and truly looked after.

Whether people opt for a leisurely breakfast, a cup of tea and a sandwich, a selection of 'cake tapas' or one of the many afternoon tea options (which range from 'traditional' right up to 'regal' with a bottle of Pol Roger Champagne), the customer service remains the same. It's all about giving people a few moments of indulgence, of being looked after and of taking time out of their normal lives for a while.

These are the 'treasured moments' that Sarah Jameson is creating in her timeless tea room – the intimate and elegant 24-seater venue is more than a place to enjoy some delicious refreshments. The vintage charm, warm hospitality and exceptionally good tea and cakes come together to create a little taste of luxury in the midst of modern life.

Jameson's Café & Tea Rooms
GOAT'S CHEESE RAREBIT

One of the most popular brunch options at Jameson's is the speciality rarebit made with goat's cheese, cheddar and red onion chutney.

Preparation time: Approx. 10 minutes | Cooking time: Approx. 5 minutes | Serves 1

Ingredients

2 slices thick white or granary bread

150g mature cheddar, grated

50g goat's cheese, crumbled

1 large egg

Cracked black pepper

2 tbsp premium quality red onion chutney

Method

Lightly toast the slices of bread. In a bowl combine the grated mature cheddar, crumbled goat's cheese and egg. Season with ground black pepper.

Spread the toast with a generous covering of the red onion chutney, then top with the cheese mixture.

Grill the rarebit until golden and serve.

Bringing brewing back to
KIRKSTALL

Kirkstall in Leeds has a brewing heritage stretching back to the 12th century and Kirkstall Brewery is reviving that proud brewing heritage.

The magnificent stone Kirkstall Brewery was built in 1833. However, the history of brewing in this spot dates back much further than that – Cistercian monks had founded an abbey on the banks of the River Aire at Kirkstall back in the 12th century, which included a brewhouse and a forge.

Kirkstall Brewery produced beer from 1833 until 1983, when it was closed down by its last owners, Whitbread. The Kirkstall Brewery beers were highly regarded throughout Yorkshire and the north-east of England and acquired a chain of tied pubs and built an impressive free-trade business. The brewery also had offices in London and exported beer to Australia and New Zealand, making use of the canal system to transport their beer to the coast for loading onto ships for export.

In 2012, there was a new chapter in the life of Kirkstall Brewery, when a smaller brewery was built in the shadows of the original, a few hundred yards down the canal. They bought a pub (Kirkstall Bridge) across the canal to showcase the beers and are very proud that in its three years of being open, it has won the 'Best Pub in Leeds' award three times, thanks to its fantastic range of beers and equally excellent food.

Kirkstall Bridge uses local Yorkshire produce and cooks all its dishes from scratch on the premises. The Sunday menu is extremely popular, especially the beef brisket which has quickly become the stuff of Leeds legend! The Scotch egg is also a winner – it's the perfect snack to accompany a pint of Kirkstall beer – along with its pizzas, which have gained quite a following.

The Kirkstall Brewery outgrew its original premises in 2015 and moved to a much larger site on Kirkstall Road, closer to the city centre. There are plans in the making for an on-site restaurant and taphouse, which (they hope!) by the time you are reading this will be fully open.

Using only the finest ingredients available and carefully combining traditional brewing methods with pioneering new techniques, they hope to make Kirkstall a revered term in the brewing world once again.

Kirkstall Brewery

KIRKSTALL RAREBIT

This is a rarebit that packs a punch – use the angriest cheddar you can find to stand up to the smoked paprika, cayenne and Dissolution Extra IPA.

Preparation time: 10 minutes | Cooking time: 15 minutes | Serves 2

Ingredients

100g pancetta, diced

½2 shallots, finely chopped

1 knob of butter

3 tsp wholemeal flour

1 tsp hot smoked paprika

½ tsp cayenne pepper

250g strong cheddar, grated

200ml Dissolution Extra IPA

4 slices Leeds Bread Co-op rye bread, toasted on one side

Method

In a dry saucepan, heat the pancetta until the fat starts to ooze. Add the shallots and cook until the pancetta is crispy and shallots are golden brown. Drain onto kitchen roll and set aside (don't clean the pan).

In the same (now empty) pan, add the butter, flour, paprika and cayenne and stir until it all comes together in to a thick roux-style paste. Cook this out for a couple of minutes.

Stir in the cheese until completely melted and, while continuously stirring, slowly dribble in the Dissolution Extra IPA (approximately 200ml – don't make it too runny).

Stir in the cooked pancetta and shallots. Once all combined, set aside to cool. This mixture will now keep in the fridge for up to a week so you'll always be ready for rarebit.

When cooled, spread the mixture thickly over the un-toasted side of the bread and place under the grill until it transforms into a golden brown volcano. Serve with mixed salad.

Enjoy (and leave the salad).

Marvellous MEAT

Based in Cleckheaton, Metcalfe's Butchers has been trading since 1962. A true family business now in the second generation of ownership, it's safe to say they know a little bit about good meat...

The finest quality meat starts with high quality animals, which is responsible sourcing, is an integral part of the Metcalfe's business. Supporting local farmers who breed happy and healthy free-range animals is the key and animal welfare is very important to John Metcalfe and his team. Highly skilled traditional butchers, the team at Metcalfe's believe that only well cared for animals, farmed with good husbandry and understanding, produce the best quality meat. Ensuring full traceability from farm to fork means customers can count on this quality each time they visit.

Everything Metcalfe's sell is made on the premises by hand, from their corned beef and free-range pork sausages to their famous stand pies. Each and every product is produced using traditional methods, with taste being a top priority! Metcalfe's enduringly popular stand pies are an example of this attention to detail. Join the back of a very long queue on Christmas Eve and you're sure to taste why! Lovingly made using the very best pork with just the right amount of jelly and a delicious rich crust, these stand pies are famous across Yorkshire. A classic Yorkshire Ploughman's dinner with a slice of stand pie, salad, pickled onions, cheese and chutney makes a tasty summer supper. At Christmas, stand pies are traditionally eaten on Boxing Day, along with the leftover turkey and an array of pickles and crusty bread; the perfect addition to any festive table. Metcalfe's have even sent a stand pie (a very large one!) all the way to Hong Kong. The pie was requested by the Hong Kong police force when sovereignty over Hong Kong was handed over to Chinese rule. The Chinese diplomats loved the stand pie so much that Metcalfe's sent another 10lb pie!

If, like the Chinese diplomats, you're a big fan of Metcalfe's stand pies, you can even have them at your wedding in place of or as well as a more conventional wedding cake. The wedding pies are custom made to each couple's requirements and can be decorated in whatever design you desire, and in colours carefully selected to match any colour scheme. Anything goes, from pastry braids and roses to lettering! Each wedding pie is unique.

Another particular Metcalfe's speciality is their free-range dry cured middle and back bacon. Produced from free-range pigs bred in the UK, the bacon is dry cured by the team on-site in Cleckheaton. Tender and sweet with just the right amount of salt and fat, this bacon is award-winning. In 2014 Metcalfe's bacon was awarded a prestigious Great Taste Award, winning three gold stars. Try it yourself as bacon should be eaten: in the perfect bacon sarnie.

Metcalfe's Butchers
PERFECT BACON SANDWICH

Bringing you the perfect bacon sandwich in under fifteen minutes.
Metcalfe's choose their finest selection of award-winning dry cured bacon and
accompany it with their speciality black pudding. A twist on a classic.

Preparation time: 5 minutes | Cooking time: 15 minutes | Serves 4

Ingredients

4 floured breadcakes

16 rashers dry cured bacon

6 tomatoes, halved

200g black pudding, sliced

Olive oil

Method

Heat the grill to a medium heat placing the bacon under for about 10 minutes, turning each rasher half way.

Meanwhile, heat a frying pan on a medium to high heat and thinly slice the black pudding, about ½cm thick. Add the black pudding to the pan, cook for 4 minutes, turning each piece half way. Next, add olive oil to the pan with the halved tomatoes and leave to cook, face side down, for 2 minutes.

Remove the bacon from the grill (when cooked to your desire) and turn off the heat from the pan. Slice the breadcakes in half and assemble each sandwich, towering the bacon, black pudding and tomatoes.

Your friendly neighbourhood KITCHEN

Welcome to Mill Kitchen – a laidback café serving up
great food made with quality ingredients.

Take a look beyond the city centre, and you'll find a plethora of community-driven, local heroes that challenge some of the city's finest establishments in terms of quality and value for money. Mill Kitchen, run by husband and wife team Tom and Ailsa, is one of those places and you'll find it in Farsley's historic Sunny Bank Mills, a heritage site with decades in the textile industry behind it. Just like the original mill, Mill Kitchen is all about using great raw materials and traditional methods to produce the best results.

"We believe strongly in honest wholesome food: food that is made with traceable, sustainable ingredients and made with care, is food that will do you good. Everything is fresh and healthy, nothing is processed and we don't take any short cuts!" says Ailsa. Most goods are made from scratch on site but things that aren't, are brought in from local people that they trust such as Leeds Bread Co-op, North Star Coffee, Cryer & Stott Cheese and Northern Bloc Ice Cream.

The Mill Kitchen chefs use the seasonal produce on offer to inspire a regularly changing menu which features plenty of substantial brunch options as well as lunch plates, skillet dishes, nourishing bowls and a daily range of fresh salads. The Mill Kitchen philosophy is all about balance, so you'll also find a wide array of baked goods expertly turned out by team star baker Nikki Glynn. Vegetarians and vegans are well catered for and there are plenty of gluten and dairy-free options too, making it easy for everyone to eat well.

Regular evening events at the venue include pop-up supper clubs by head chef and Masterchef: The Professionals contestant Ben Keay consisting of a seven-course tasting menu to excite the senses. There's also a monthly family supper where parents who miss eating out can bring their kids to enjoy a special play area and informal family friendly meal.

It's not just the locals seeking their avocado toast fix anymore; with 2016 bringing a nomination for 'Best Coffee Shop' in the Leeds Lifestyle Awards and a four-star-review in the Yorkshire Evening Post, the Mill Kitchen continues to go from strength to strength.

If you haven't visited Farsley, or the Mill Kitchen, a warm welcome awaits.

MILL KITCHEN

Mill Kitchen

Seeded sourdough 3.20

Almond... 1.50

Mill Kitchen
RASPBERRY CHEESECAKE BROWNIE

This brownie is an amalgamation of our original brownie, adapted from a Hugh Fearnley-Whittingstall recipe and a cheesecake swirl brownie. We have played around with it and made it gluten-free. The browned butter and high level of cocoa makes the brownie incredibly rich and the cheesecake, with its subtle tang of goat's cheese, sets it off perfectly. You can use any seasonal fruit – cherries and blackcurrants are also delicious.

Preparation time: 30 minutes | Cooking time: 45 minutes | Serves 12-16

Ingredients

For the fruit:

1 tbsp brandy

150g raspberries

For the brownie:

180g butter

3 eggs

300g light brown sugar

1 tsp vanilla extract

100g cocoa powder

50g ground almonds

Pinch of salt

100g dark chocolate, chopped

For the cheesecake:

240g cream cheese

120g goat's cheese, mild

30g butter

1 egg

45g caster sugar

Method

For the fruit

Start by stirring the brandy into the raspberries; leave them to macerate while you prepare the brownie mixture.

For the brownie

Preheat the oven to 180°c and grease a 24 x 24cm square tin with butter.

Brown the butter over a high heat in a saucepan; you are looking for it to go a golden brown colour and smell nutty and delicious (rather than just like hot melted butter). Keep an eye on it as it can bubble over easily!

Meanwhile, beat the eggs and sugar together in a food mixer or with an electric whisk until the mixture is thick and pale and starting to hold its shape as it leaves the whisk.

When the butter is ready, take it off the heat and add the vanilla. Pour this into the egg and sugar mix and beat it all together.

In a separate bowl whisk together the cocoa powder, ground almonds and salt to remove any lumps.

Add the dry ingredients to the wet and combine well (you can be quite vigorous).

Finally, stir in the chocolate and pour the brownie mixture into the tin.

For the cheesecake

For the cheesecake mix, beat everything together (again easier with a food mixer or electric whisk) until thick and smooth. Fold in the raspberries just enough to get a ripple effect. Spoon the cheesecake mixture over the brownie and swirl together with the point of a knife.

Bake in the oven for 30-45 minutes; as it's quite a wet mixture it will take longer and look more cooked than a typical brownie - you want it to be set and not wobbly when you take it out.

This brownie is best served chilled; it will keep in the fridge for approximately 5 days.

Moosic
TO OUR EARS

The Moody Cow takes pride in sourcing and serving the finest locally grown, raised and reared produce to celebrate the goodness that comes from God's own county.

The independently owned steakhouse, bar and grill is the result of years of planning for James Boshier and Martin Oates. They noticed a distinct lack of restaurants that you could go to for quality meat and steak so they put their heads together to build this project. "We did this a little differently, instead of finding the restaurant and then figuring out what to do next, we saw what we wanted on the plate and worked our way backwards from there," said James.

Months of research went into finding the right rare breed cattle for their restaurant, they wanted to make sure all their beef was fully traceable and raised and reared in Yorkshire. The menu is locally sourced where possible and hand-picked to ensure consistent quality and freshness, fish from the Yorkshire coast, chicken from a local farmer and vegetables grown just a few miles away, they even sourced their cow-hide seats!

Hearty appetites are well catered for with their meaty sharing platters such as their tomahawk bone in ribeye steak, the chateaubriand tenderloin fillet and their steak taster board which consists of cuts of sirloin, rump and ribeye. Their beef is always dry aged for a minimum of 28 days to ensure every succulent steak is at its optimum quality when going on the plate.

If you're not a meat lover, they deviate from that as well with lots of fish, pasta and vegetarian dishes as well as a specials board which changes every two weeks, appealing to a wide spectrum of tastes.

While they don't claim to be the cheapest restaurant around, the dishes represent terrific value for money and it's worth getting a drink or two to wash it all down from the extensive wine list while there's a well-stocked bar with a range of American and continental beers as well as spirits to shake up your classic cocktail of choice.

Both partners live locally and the passion has spread as both families participate in growing the business, including their kids who have worked their way through the ranks at The Moody Cow.

They have grown a steady following which has helped them gain recognition from the H&N Magazine EAT Awards and the Yorkshire Evening Post Oliver Awards.

The Yorkshire born and bred boys are very strong-minded about this venture and with two venues in their herd already, they're looking to expand into hopefully a dozen sites within Yorkshire in the next few years.

THE TOMAHAWK SHARING BOARD

The tomahawk is a large bone in ribeye steak that usually weighs between 20 and 40 ounces. The meat is tender and well marbled, and the steak's frenched bone along with all the other components makes for very impressive presentation.

Preparation time: 40 minutes | Cooking time: 4 hours and 20 minutes | Serves 2

Ingredients

28oz dry aged rare breed bone in ribeye steak

For the braised beef shin and bone marrow canoe:

Splash of olive oil

2 red onions, peeled & chopped

3 carrots, peeled & chopped

3 sticks of celery, trimmed & chopped

4 garlic cloves, unpeeled

3 sprigs fresh rosemary

2 bay leaves

Small handful of dried porcini

1 cinnamon stick

1kg quality shin of beef, bone removed and trimmed

1 tbsp plain flour

800g good-quality tinned plum tomatoes

500ml quality red wine

Pinch of salt and black pepper

For the bone marrow sauce:

2 litres beef stock

100g unsalted butter

250g peeled and finely sliced shallot (approx. 5 banana shallots)

150g white wine

100g Dijon mustard

10ml sherry vinegar

15ml lemon juice

100g bone marrow, rinsed and diced

Sprinkling of chopped fine herbs like parsley

For garnish:

12 girolle mushrooms

6 shallots, cut into rings

Pinch of fresh baby nettles

Method

For the braised beef shin and bone marrow canoe

Preheat your oven to 180°c/Gas 4.

In a heavy-bottomed ovenproof saucepan, heat a splash of olive oil and gently fry the onions, carrots, celery, garlic, herbs, porcini and cinnamon for 5 minutes until softened slightly.

Meanwhile, toss the pieces of beef in a little seasoned flour, shaking off any excess. Add the meat to the pan and stir everything together before adding the tomatoes, wine and a pinch of salt and pepper.

Gently bring to the boil, cover with a double-thickness piece of tinfoil and a lid, then place in your preheated oven for 3 hours or until the beef is tender and can be broken up with a spoon. Remember to taste and check the seasoning, then remove the cinnamon stick and rosemary sprigs and serve in your split bone marrow canoe.

For the bone marrow sauce

Pour the beef stock into a large saucepan and place over a high heat. Bring to the boil and allow the liquid to reduce by three-quarters until 500ml remains (approximately 25 minutes).

In the meantime, melt the butter in a medium saucepan and cook the shallots for approximately 7–10 minutes until they are light brown in colour. Add the wine and allow to reduce by three-quarters.

Remove the shallot pan from the heat and add the Dijon mustard. Stir thoroughly before adding the reduced beef stock, sherry vinegar and lemon juice. Gently heat the sauce and when hot, add the diced bone marrow and remove the pan from the heat - the bone marrow should soften but not melt.

Stir the chopped herbs into the sauce and season with salt and freshly ground pepper before pouring into a warm jug.

For the steak

Remove the steak from the fridge 20 minutes prior to cooking and let it come to room temperature.

Wrap the exposed rib bone with a damp paper towel and then cover the bone completely with heavy-duty foil to shield it from scorching.

Season the meat with sea salt and pepper and sear over a high direct heat for four minutes on each side before moving to a heavy bottom griddle pan or frying pan. This will lock in the juices and the flavour. Your target temperature (using a meat thermometer inserted into the thickest part of the cut) is 55°c for medium-rare, 65°c for medium and 75°c for medium-well.

Lightly fry the girolle mushrooms in butter for 5 minutes and deep fry the shallots.

Once the meat has rested for 3-5 minutes, start plating by thickly slicing and pouring over any remaining juices from the pan. Lay the mushrooms and shallot rings on the meat and sprinkle with baby nettles.

Nobody does it BETTER

Mr Nobody is the tale of three friends expressing their passion and ideas to take you on a journey of discovery and deliciousness, with a welcome that nobody can match.

Everyone at Mr Nobody has the same mindset; to continue developing and never stand still. The restaurant and cocktail bar is a sustainable project with an aim to grow into something really special. The focus is on constant growth, refining the details and using carefully selected products and yes they are guilty of not talking about them enough, but that's kind of the point of Mr Nobody!

Their extensive list of wine, fizz and cocktails might be just what you need after a hard day at work. You'll find the drinks that everyone knows and loves but without all the smoke and mirrors, as well as a unique cocktail list written with a view to test the boundaries of mixology. Andy the barman owns a drinks company which luckily for you, means he has access to some truly rare and interesting concoctions – which is their secret weapon.

For some nibbles to accompany your drink, have a gander at their bar snacks menu which features a gourmet style toastie, think braised shin of beef in beer with caramelised onions, toasted in a freshly made English butter brioche! Get it while you can though because the great thing about Mr Nobody is that the menu could change at any moment, John the chef likes to mix things up, as and when he feels, to keep things fresh and interesting.

The same goes for downstairs in the cellar restaurant where you'll have to book in advance for a tasting style menu. This is because they buy in the ingredients for who they've got booked in each day and no more than that. This allows them to serve food at its pinnacle of freshness. Each night their fridges are empty so it's sustainable, ethical, responsible and most importantly – delicious.

The team are not known for taking something out of the book of normality, but for challenging the perception and taking it up a notch with different textures and deeper dimensions. "I want to be able to share great food that I have discovered myself with everyone else – I love experimenting with different cultures and cuisines. This is the place where people who have an interest in food can discover and try things they haven't tried before, or try the best version of the thing they love most, without having to pay extortionate prices," says John.

Mr Nobody is creating a loyal tribe of followers but at the rate that these guys are going, you'll have to follow closely if you want to keep up!

Mr Nobody
CHOCOLATE WITH LEMON, BANANA AND COCONUT

I love chocolate and coconut, this is the perfect dish to end on at Mr Nobody's, something chocolatey and light yet heavy on textures.

Preparation time: 1 hour plus cooling time | Cooking time: 2 hours | Serves 12

Ingredients

1 jar of lemon curd
24 squares of chocolate sponge cake
12 quenelles of chocolate ice cream

For the chocolate sauce:
120g caster sugar
120ml water
40g cocoa powder
100g whipping cream

For the digestive tuile:
115g digestive biscuits
75g icing sugar
25g plain flour
2 egg whites
50g butter

For the rice crispy cake:
15g of best quality dark chocolate
10g rice crispies

For the coconut mousse:
125ml of fresh young coconut juice and innards

For the banana foam:
60ml milk
125ml whipping cream
1 tbsp banana purée
1 tbsp icing sugar

For the nougatine with cocoa nibs:
45g caster sugar
1g apple pectin
30g butter
12g glucose
1 tsp water
45g cocoa nibs

For the chocolate crème fraiche:
250g crème fraiche or yoghurt
160g milk chocolate

For the chocolate opaline:
55g wet fondant
35g glucose
5g 70% dark chocolate

Method

For the chocolate sauce

Place sugar, water and cocoa powder into a pan and bring to the boil. Add the whipping cream and bring back to the boil before simmering until the desired consistency is reached. Pass through a sieve and chill.

For the digestive tuille

Blitz all together and spread a thin layer of the mixture on a baking sheet, bake at 150°c for 4-5 minutes.

For the rice crispy cake

Melt the chocolate over a bain marie then stir in the rice crispies before putting in the fridge to set.

For the coconut mousse

Blitz all together and pass through a fine sieve, add to a whipping syphon and charge with one N20 to keep light, alternatively gently whip after passing and place in a piping bag.

For the banana foam

Mix everything until smooth and set the foam in a whipping syphon.

For the nougatine with cocoa nibs

Preheat the oven to 190°c.

In a saucepan combine the sugar, pectin, butter, glucose and water and cook over a low heat until the mixture is smooth, then add the cocoa nibs.

Drop into 5p sized mounds or circles on a baking sheet leaving a gap between them so they don't merge together. Bake for 10 minutes.

For the chocolate crème fraiche:

Warm the crème fraîche in a saucepan and add the chocolate, stir well until melted.

For the chocolate opaline

Heat the pouring fondant and the glucose to 155°c, incorporate the chopped chocolate and pour onto a tray. Leave to cool, and then break up into smaller pieces before blitzing into a powder.

Sift the powder onto a baking sheet using a stencil if you wish, then bake at 160°c until holes have formed. Cool and store in an air tight container.

To assemble

We don't really have any rules on plating up, we like to showcase the food in a neat and tidy way – just have fun with it!

Brewing REVOLUTION

Northern Monk takes the knowledge from monastic brewing's past and combines it with 21st-century advancements in the craft to create innovative brews that will continue to stand the test of time.

Founded in 2013, Northern Monk Brew Co. initially operated as a "cuckoo" brewery (meaning they brewed their beers from other breweries by contract) until they established a nest to call their own in 2014. This home was a derelict Grade II-listed flax store building in Holbeck, which incidentally is known as the cradle of the industrial revolution.

The first floor houses the brewery itself where they brew award-winning craft beers such as their flagship beer Eternal Session IPA, which took home the bronze medal in its category at the World Beer Cup 2016. The second floor is home to The Refectory taproom and kitchen, where brunch, lunch, small plates and mains are crafted as carefully as the beers using local produce and creative cooking. Dishes are happily paired with one of their beers – and often are cooked using them, too. The third floor Chapter Hall is the event space where parties, fairs and weddings make the most of this unique industrial building.

The history of monastic brewing is at the heart of things at Northern Monk, as the name suggests. They have taken thousands of years of tradition and heritage (brewing is recorded in Yorkshire as far back as the Domesday book) and used it alongside forward-thinking innovations and a progressive approach to ingredients and techniques.

They have been growing to such an extent that they are expanding into a second brewing site to increase their core production. The Old Flax Store will then become home to their new arm Refectory Brew Co., which will be dedicated to more experimental brewing, creative collaborations and passion projects.

With head brewer Brian Dickson having a degree in music composition and lead brewer Dave Kerr previously working as a biochemist, the pair have come together with an unstoppable art-meets-science force that has led to the creation of some truly cutting edge beers. They also collaborate with many like-minded businesses and artists (both in and out of the brewing industry) on an infinite journey of learning and creativity. From legendary Swedish progressive metal band Opeth to The Real Junk Food Project (an organisation whose mission is to repurpose food waste), Northern Monk Brew Co. transcend any preconceived notions of the drinks industry on their quest to support and showcase like-minded creatives who share their vision of craftsmanship, quality and appreciation of timeless design.

Northern Monk Brew Co.
HANGER STEAK

A cut of beef with fabulous flavour, we serve hanger steak with pumpkin purée, girolles, grilled radicchio and Northern Monk Chennai jus. Pair it perfectly with Northern Monk Dark Arches Black IPA.

Preparation time: Approx. 30 minutes | Cooking time: Approx. 30 minutes | Serves 4

Ingredients

For the Chennai jus:

250ml fresh beef stock

10g cornflour

100ml Northern Monk Chennai Export Porter

Salt and pepper

For the pumpkin purée:

250g pumpkin, peeled and cubed

400ml vegetable stock

1 tsp honey

Salt

For the garnishes:

30g chives, finely chopped

500ml extra virgin rapeseed oil, plus 1 teaspoon

50g walnuts

1 small bunch of sage

Salt

For the hanger steak:

4 x 7oz. hanger steaks

2 tbsp extra virgin rapeseed oil

Salt and pepper

For the girolles and grilled radicchio:

50g girolle mushrooms

1 radicchio lettuce

Extra virgin rapeseed oil

Salt and pepper

Method

For the Chennai jus

In heavy-based saucepan, bring the beef stock to simmer and reduce by half. Mix the cornflour with a few tablespoons of cold water to form a loose paste. Add the paste and Northern Monk Chennai to the beef stock and reduce by half again. Season to taste and keep warm.

For the pumpkin purée

Add the pumpkin and vegetable stock to a heavy-based saucepan and bring to boil. Once boiling, lower the heat and simmer until the pumpkin is soft enough for a knife to slip through with ease. Drain and reserve the liquid. Blend the pumpkin with a little of the reserved liquid to achieve a purée. Add the honey and salt. Continue blending until glossy and smooth. Keep warm.

For the garnishes

Preheat the oven to 200°c. Make a chive oil by blitzing the finely chopped chives with 200ml rapeseed oil until fully combined (about 1 minute). Season lightly with salt. Make a walnut crumb by coating the walnuts in 1 tsp rapeseed oil and toast in the preheated oven for 3-4 minutes. Roughly blitz to course breadcrumb consistency. Sprinkle in 1 tsp salt and set aside. Make some sage crisps by heating about 300ml rapeseed oil in a small saucepan over medium-high heat until hot. Fry 6-8 sage leaves at a time until crisp (2–3 seconds). Transfer with a fork to paper towels and sprinkle generously with salt.

For the hanger steaks

Preheat the oven to 200°c. Leave the hanger steaks in cool area for at least 30 minutes to reach room temperature. Coat the steaks in rapeseed oil and place in very hot frying pan. Fry the steaks for 1-2 minutes each side (enough for a good brown surface). Then, place in the oven for 5-7 minutes. Season to taste and rest for 5-7 minutes while you prepare the girolles and radicchio.

For the girolles and radicchio

Trim any visible grit from mushrooms and fry in 2 tablespoons of rapeseed oil over gentle heat for 3-4 minutes. Season to taste. Trim and discard any outer leaves from the radicchio. Quarter the lettuce head, drizzle with rapeseed oil and season. Grill for 3-4 minutes.

To assemble and serve

While the radicchio and girolles cook, slice the steaks to your desired thickness. Settle a spoonful of purée onto the plate and add the radicchio. Arrange the steaks over the radicchio and scatter the girolles over. Sprinkle over some walnut crumb, drizzle with chive oil and decorate with a few sage crisps. Serve the Chennai jus on the side.

Out of the woods and into THE CITY

Out of the Woods was established in 2006 and was born out of a long term desire from Ross Stringer to own her own business.

Ten years ago there wasn't much choice when it came to getting quality 'fast food' that wasn't from a chain, it was pretty much Pret a Manger or nothing. Frustrated with the lack of options, Ross Stringer went on a mission to change that and now along with her tight team of six, they keep the two carefully chosen sites in Holbeck Urban Village and Granary Wharf running smoothly.

Squirrels, owls and hedgehogs are dotted around the room of reclaimed wood panels and you can't ignore the extraordinary collection of light bulbs hanging down from the ceiling. The woodland-esque setting is a warm welcome to cyclists, commuters and dog walkers who have either popped in for a bite or grabbing a coffee to go.

Creating exciting, healthy and delicious food and drink is what they do and they have done it exceptionally well with the help of some fantastic local suppliers. Dark Woods Coffee, Gilchrists Bakery, Acorn Dairies and Brown & Blond have worked closely with Ross to bring the best offering to create a mouth-watering menu of sandwiches, soups, salads and savouries. Everything is freshly prepared and nothing is processed so you can eat your meals guilt-free and have room for something sweet too, perhaps a brownie or a slab of sea salted caramel millionaire shortbread.

Their Yorkshire roast ham sandwich with cheese, wholegrain mustard, spinach and homemade tomato chutney is a bestseller at the café. "My mum used to make the chutney when I was little and she kept the recipe a secret until I grew up so now I get to share its deliciousness with everybody!" says Ross. Keep an eye on the specials board as it changes every week and features oozy grilled cheeses and comforting bowls of seasonal soup.

From espressos to mochas, raising the standards of their coffee was an executive decision that Ross made for the better - now 50% of their sales are for coffee and served by fully trained baristas. Their smoothies and juices are also a winner for those who want a bit of a boost but if you're after something a little more substantial, head to the Granary Wharf site for Saturday brunch – expect Belgian waffles with bacon and maple syrup and eggy bread with bacon, spinach and chilli chutney.

Out of The Woods pride themselves on recognising repeat customers and with the level of food and drink that they are serving, it's no wonder that they keep coming back.

Out of the Woods
BRAZILIAN BREAKFAST

The flavour of acai has been described as a mix of chocolate and blueberries...
but here's the best bit. It's really good for you! Acai has been shown in
laboratory analysis to have higher antioxidant levels than blueberries,
pomegranates or red wine. In addition, it is unique among fruit in that it
contains healthy omega oils (6 and 9). Pure acai can be difficult to source, but
is worth the effort. You cannot make this recipe with anything other than pure
acai pulp which is top grade and has not been processed – just simply flash
frozen. It is also vegan friendly!

Preparation time: 10 minutes | Serves 1

Ingredients

100g frozen acai berry pulp

30ml guarana syrup

150ml milk, non-dairy

1 banana

85g good quality granola

Handful of fresh fruit

Method

First blend the acai berry pulp, guarana syrup, non-dairy milk and half of the banana in a blender, until it is a yoghurt-like consistency.

Pour the blended mixture into a bowl and top with the granola.

Cut your fresh fruit and the other half of the banana (you can use any fresh fruit) and arrange on top of the granola.

Enjoy with a spoon!

Taste THE TWIST

Designed to delight the taste buds, ProperMaid supply caterers, cafés and retailers with innovative handmade cakes with a twist.

The concept of ProperMaid began when keen baker Allison Whitmarsh was asked to start up a hypothetical business project when she went back to university aged 40. Just five days after finishing her degree, she sold her baked goods at her first farmers market and it took off from there!

She spent the first six months working from home with the aid of school kitchens to bake in bulk for big events. Outgrowing that, she bought a small retail shop just up the road to convert into a bakery, now they are based in two factories that will soon be merged into one big one. ProperMaid is known for their innovative and unusual cake flavours, such as courgette and lime, beetroot and white chocolate and Huddersfield-inspired dandelion and burdock, the last recipe won a Great Taste 2012 Gold Award and you can find it overleaf.

The key to ProperMaid's success is their passion for 'proper' ingredients, you won't find any artificial ingredients or preservatives, and everything is locally sourced if possible. Their 'Made Without' range is a huge hit with the customers and they do a selection of cookies and scones too.

"Ever since BBC's Great British Bake Off, people are wanting something different. There is a huge market for homemade cakes now and we stand out because we can manufacture these exactly how you would make them at home, but in bulk. No machines. And we'll never change that no matter how big we get," says Allison.

You'll find these properly made cakes flying off the shelves in businesses and cafés across the whole of England, including popular stores Fenwick, Pret A Manger and Ocado.

Allison gets inspiration from her everyday life as a foodie, even savoury dishes play a part in her ideas for flavours. This is how the carrot cake with yuzu icing came about and the eminent Christmas dinner cake which won the attention of Dragons' Den investor Deborah Meaden. Since then ProperMaid has gone on to win numerous accolades including the Great Taste Awards, Baking Industry Awards and their most recent one at the Yorkshire Powerhouse Business Awards for International Trade.

The leading manufacturer of flavours has shook up the industry for cake connoisseurs nationally, ProperMaid hopes to set the bar abroad too.

Proper Maid
DANDELION & BURDOCK CAKE

This recipe was developed as a tribute to Huddersfield using the iconic Ben Shaws brand. It became our signature cake and has gone on to win two awards – best bakery product at the Deliciously Yorkshire Awards and a gold star at the Great Taste Awards 2011. We still sell this cake today and it's now one of our top ten best selling cakes!

Preparation time: 30 minutes | Cooking time: 45 minutes | Serves 8

Ingredients

For the sponge:

185g self-raising flour

105g soft vegetable margarine, preferably 80% fat content

185g caster sugar

25g cocoa powder

5g bicarbonate of soda

85ml milk

165ml dandelion & burdock pop (half a can)

2 eggs

For the icing:

20g vegetable margarine, softened

130g icing sugar

10g cocoa powder

20ml dandelion & burdock pop

Method

For the sponge

Preheat the oven at 160°c/Gas 3.

Grease and line a 18cm, round spring-form cake tin.

Rub together the flour, margarine, caster sugar, cocoa powder and bicarbonate sugar until it resembles fine breadcrumbs.

Gradually add the milk and the dandelion & burdock pop (reserving 20ml for the icing) followed by the eggs. Beat together until a thick smooth batter consistency is achieved.

Pour the cake batter into the cake tin and bake in the oven for approximately 40 minutes until it is firm to the touch and when inserted with a cake skewer comes out clean.

For the icing

Beat together the soft margarine and icing sugar until smooth.

Add the cocoa powder and dandelion & burdock pop you reserved earlier and mix until well combined.

Spread onto the flat side of the cake and sprinkle with some icing sugar to serve!

The Queen o' t'
SUNDAY ROAST

A modern dining pub in South Milford, The Queen o' t' owd Thatch has been gradually building up a reputation as one of the best places to eat in West Yorkshire... with its Sunday lunches in particular creating quite a stir.

An affinity for pubs runs in the blood for Kirsty, who has been running The Queen o' t' owd Thatch with her partner Annie since 2013. Her grandfather had run a pub and her father was a master brewer, so she grew up in and around the industry. She got her first job as a pot washer at the age of 15 and from there she worked in every type of venue imaginable – from small local inns to fine dining establishments – her career has taken her all over the country.

When she met Annie, a passionate foodie and gardener, they discovered a joint ambition of running their own pub. Four years later Annie left her successful career in charities behind and they gravitated back to Kirsty's Yorkshire roots to run The Queen o' t' owd Thatch in South Milford.

The place became a symbol of everything they loved in a pub – cosy, friendly and with quality food and drink for diners, drinkers and dogs to all enjoy, with a stylish beer garden to boot. Kirsty describes Annie, who manages front of house, as "the friendliest person you can ever meet." Guests can choose anything from the menu to be served up in smaller portions. If you see things on the menu that might tempt the tiniest tots, the kitchen are happy to put it together – a little mash with some gravy and carrots? No problem.

The drinks are as important as the food, and they serve only those beers, wines and cocktails they enjoy themselves. Like everything else, if Annie and Kirsty don't believe in it, it doesn't make the cut.

However it's the food that has really helped this pub make a name for itself. It was nominated for Yorkshire Life's Dining Pub of the Year in its debut year and has been listed as a runner up for an astounding three consecutive years for the Observer Food Monthly Award for Best Sunday Lunch. The produce generally comes from within 20 miles – and some of it from Annie's kitchen garden (from herbs to new potatoes, turnips and runner beans) or from customers who have had a glut of produce in their gardens.

The backbone of their business comes from their amazing bunch of regulars, Annie and Kirsty are equally excited to welcome guests who have begun seeking them out from further afield. As Kirsty says, "people in Yorkshire don't mind travelling for good food, especially a good roast!"

Queen o' t' owd Thatch
SEA BASS FILLET WITH BISQUE SAUCE AND PICKLED MUSSELS

The amazing flavour of the sauce is down to the stock made with langoustine shells. You could use a packet of frozen shell-on prawns instead, if you like, but your fishmonger should be able to order langoustine shells for you. Use thick line-caught sea bass fillets.

Preparation time: Approx. 30 minutes, plus 1 hour pickling and 1 hour infusing stock
| Cooking time: Approx. 2 hours | Serves: 4

Ingredients

4 sea bass fillets

Cooked greens, buttered

Maldon sea salt

Vegetable oil and butter

For the mussels:

28 large mussels

1 clove garlic, thinly sliced

1 shallot, thinly sliced

40g caster sugar

15g Maldon sea salt

1 bay leaf

175ml cider vinegar

½ tsp each fennel and coriander seeds

75ml medium white wine

For the bisque sauce:

500g langoustine shells

500g crab legs

1 large onion, sliced

2 carrots, chopped

1 bulb fennel, sliced

1 bulb garlic, chopped

8 sprigs thyme

4 bay leaves

1 tsp each dulce and picante pimentón

35ml each brandy and Pernod

75ml Noilly Prat

30ml medium white wine

100g tomato purée

200g each white and brown crab meat

Method

For the mussels

Scrub and de-beard the mussels, rinse well and set aside. Place all the other ingredients except the mussels and wine in a pan with 500ml water and bring to the boil. Simmer for 10 minutes. Remove from the heat and cover to infuse for 30 minutes. Strain and cool.

Place the mussels in a bowl with the wine and a pinch of sea salt. Place a large heavy saucepan with a tight fitting lid on a high heat and, when hot, tip the mussels, wine and salt into it and replace the lid quickly. Shake and leave for a couple of minutes until all the mussels have opened. Strain the mussels and retain the liquid. Discard any mussels that haven't opened.

When they are cool, pick the flesh from the shells and add to the cooled pickling liquor. Leave for 1 hour.

For the bisque

Start by making a shell stock. Roast the langoustine shells and crab legs in a hot oven for 15 minutes. Transfer to a saucepan, cover with cold water and bring to the boil. Skim off any residue. Add the reserved mussel juices and simmer for 20 minutes. Take off the heat and infuse for 1 hour.

Once it has infused, begin making the bisque. In a large, heavy pan heat 35ml vegetable oil on a medium heat. Cook the vegetables and herbs until soft and the onions start to caramelise. Add both types of pimentón and turn heat to high, stirring so you don't burn it. Add the brandy, Pernod, Noilly Prat and wine, and boil until almost evaporated. Keep stirring. Turn the heat to medium, add the tomato purée and cook for 5 minutes. Add the crab meats and the strained shell stock. Bring to the boil, then simmer for 1 hour. Blend the bisque to a smooth, thick soup and season with salt whilst warm. Keep warm.

To serve

Score the sea bass skin four times and season with crushed Maldon salt. Season the flesh side and rest flesh-side down for 5 minutes. Drizzle vegetable oil in a cold non-stick frying pan and place the fish in skin-side down. Put onto a medium-low heat and leave until the fish is white half way up the flesh. Check the skin – if it's crispy, flip the fish and turn up the heat. If not, keep on the skin side until it is. Once turned, throw a knob of butter in the pan. Baste the skin with the butter, working quickly to avoid burning the butter. Remove from the pan and drain on kitchen paper. Drain the mussels on kitchen paper.

Place the warm bisque in a warmed wide bowl with some hot buttered greens in the centre. Place the sea bass on top and dot pickled mussels around the edge in the sauce.

Yorkshire WAGYU

The story of Stockdales of Yorkshire is one which ties together farming and food to deliver an exceptional dining experience.

Although it opened its doors for the first time in September 2015, Stockdales of Yorkshire has links to the area's history of farming that go back decades. They work with the country's largest certified Wagyu cattle herd, which is hand-selected, aged for 28 days, precision-trimmed and cooked with the care it deserves over their Josper Grill.

Wagyu is a Japanese breed of cow which has extra fat running through the muscles, rather than just on the outside. Historically this meant that they were used for pulling carts and ploughs, but for chefs it means they have much more marbling in the meat for juicier and more flavoursome results. Their herd is raised mainly around York and never leaves the county, from farm to fork! When the steak hits the plate at Stockdales it is the final part of the perfect Yorkshire process which focuses on the welfare of animal, the care of the farmer, the diligence of the preparation, and, of course, the skill of the chef.

The restaurant has become well known for its expertly cooked steaks – the charcoal Josper Grill heats to 480°c so the meat is sealed quickly to lock in flavour and juices. The Wagyu ribeye, côte de boeuf and chateaubriand are always popular, but there is much more to Stockdales than just exceptional beef. The fish, which comes from Hodgson's Fish (who have been selling fresh seafood from East Yorkshire since 1912) is a firm favourite along with chicken and pork which comes from Sykes Farm near Wetherby.

Vegetarians don't miss out on exquisite local fare, with dishes like poached duck egg with wild mushrooms and truffle hollandaise, Harrogate blue soufflé with red wine poached pear and chicory and walnut salad. For dessert, the likes of sticky toffee pudding served with an amazing black treacle ice cream can always tempt people to find space after their main course.

They also offer a cheese board (mainly from Yorkshire, of course, but with some of the best cheeses the rest of the country has to offer) which can be paired with a wine flight – taster samples of some of their favourite wines which get fuller in body as flavour as the cheeses get stronger! The perfect end to the perfect meal.

Stockdales of Yorkshire
FILLET STEAK TARTARE, 'UMAMI YOLK', SOURDOUGH TOAST

Steak tartare is taken to new levels by using the highest quality local beef from farmers we know personally. Use the best beef possible at home for the tastiest results.

Preparation time: 15 minutes, plus 2 hours curing | Serves 4

Ingredients

For the steak tartare:

500g beef fillet, finely diced

1 shallot, finely diced

1 gherkin, finely diced

1 tbsp baby capers

60ml tomato ketchup

1 tbsp Dijon mustard

Worcestershire sauce and Tabasco, to taste

Salt, to season

For the umami yolks:

4 egg yolks

Dark soy sauce

To serve:

Sourdough toast

Method

For the umami yolks

Start by making the umami yolks. Place the egg yolks in a small dish and add enough dark soy sauce to cover. Leave to cure for 2 hours.

For the steak tartare

To assemble the tartare place the beef fillet in a bowl, add all the other ingredients and the Worcestershire sauce and Tabasco to taste, season with sea salt.

To serve

Divide the tartare onto plates and serve a drained egg yolk on top. Serve with sourdough toast on the side.

Stockdales of Yorkshire
WAGYU BEEF CHEEK BOURGUIGNON, CRISPY BACON, RED WINE SHALLOTS AND CREAMED MASH

Hearty, warming and packed full of flavour, this dish showcases our Wagyu beef, which is hand-selected, aged for up to 28 days and precision-trimmed.

Preparation time: 15 minutes | Cooking time: 4 hours – 4 hours 30 minutes | Serves 4

Ingredients

For the beef cheeks:

4 Wagyu beef cheeks, trimmed

1 onion, roughly chopped

4 garlic cloves

300ml red wine

1 litre beef stock

Small bunch thyme

2 bay leaves

30g butter

For the red wine shallots:

4 large banana shallots, peeled and halved

1 tbsp sugar

A few thyme leaves

1 bay leaf

6 black peppercorns

Red wine, to cover

For the bacon crisps:

8 rashers streaky bacon

To serve:

Creamed mashed potatoes

1 tbsp sherry vinegar

500g chestnut mushrooms

Vegetable oil, for cooking

Method

For the beef cheeks

Preheat the oven to 150°c. Heat a large ovenproof pan with some vegetable oil, add the beef cheeks and brown all over for approximately 10 minutes. Add the onion and garlic and cook for a further 5 minutes. Deglaze the pan with the red wine and add the beef stock and herbs. Place a lid on the pan and cook in the oven for 3-4 hours or until the cheeks are very tender.

For the red wine shallots

Place the shallots, sugar, herbs and peppercorns in a pan. Add just enough red wine to cover, bring to a simmer and cook gently for 30 minutes until the shallots are tender.

For the bacon crisps

Preheat the oven to 180°c. Place the bacon rashers on a parchment-lined baking tray, cover with another piece of parchment and place another baking tray on top. Cook in the oven for 15 minutes or until the bacon is crisp. Leave to cool

To finish and serve

Strain the cooking liquid from the cheeks into another pan and bring to the boil again. Whisk in a small knob of butter and a splash of sherry vinegar and add the cheeks back in to glaze them up. Lightly brush the chestnut mushrooms with oil and grill them.

Strain the red wine from the shallots into another small pan, discarding the herbs and peppercorns. Add the shallots and place on high heat until the wine has reduced and coated the shallots.

Place a beef cheek on top of some creamy mash, spoon the sauce over and garnish with bacon crisps, red wine shallots and chestnut mushrooms.

Stockdales of Yorkshire

PISTACHIO CAKE, BALSAMIC-ROASTED STRAWBERRIES AND STRAWBERRY & ELDERFLOWER SORBET

Sweet and savoury tastes combine in a medley of beautiful colours, textures and flavours. There will be plenty of pistachio cake left over to enjoy another day!

Preparation time: 30 minutes, plus churning and freezing | Cooking time: 30 minutes | Serves 4

Ingredients

For the pistachio cake:

125ml pomace oil

200g pistachios

50g polenta

1 lemon and 1 orange, zest and juice

3 eggs

200g caster sugar

100g butter, melted

75g plain flour

1 tsp baking powder

For the balsamic strawberries:

12 strawberries

50ml aged balsamic vinegar

30g icing sugar

For the Chantilly cream:

150ml whipping cream

1 vanilla pod

40g caster sugar

For the black pepper tuile:

50g isomalt

50g glucose

Freshly ground black pepper

For the sorbet:

175ml water

125g caster sugar

25g glucose

500g strawberry purée

75ml elderflower cordial

Method

For the pistachio cake

Preheat the oven to 170°c. In a blender blitz the pomace oil, pistachios, polenta, zest and juice from the orange and lemon until you have a smooth paste. In a bowl whisk the eggs and sugar until pale, then fold in the pistachio paste, stir in the butter and finally fold in the flour and baking powder. Pour into a greaseproof paper-lined cake tin (about 32 x 26cm) and bake for 20 minutes or until a skewer comes out clean.

For the balsamic strawberries

Preheat the oven to 150°c. Hull the strawberries and place in a small baking dish. Drizzle with the balsamic vinegar and dust over the icing sugar. Bake for 10 minutes and reserve the balsamic juice left in the tray.

For the Chantilly cream

Whisk the whipping cream and sugar in a bowl until you have soft peaks. Scrape the seeds from the vanilla pod, add to the cream and mix through.

For the black pepper tuile

Place the isomalt and glucose in a small saucepan. Put over medium heat and cook until it reaches 160°c on a sugar thermometer. Pour straight onto a silicone mat-lined baking tray and leave to cool. When it has cooled and hardened, place in a blender and blitz to a fine powder. Using a fine sieve, dust the sugar onto a silicone mat-lined baking tray in a fine layer. Grind fresh black pepper over the top and place in a 130°c oven with the fan off for 30 seconds-1 minute until the sugar melts again. Leave to cool.

For the sorbet

Make a stock syrup by bringing the water, sugar and glucose to a boil. Take off the heat and leave to cool. Stir in the strawberry purée and elderflower cordial, transfer to an ice cream machine and churn until just set. Transfer to the freezer.

To assemble

Cut the pistachio cake into portions and warm slightly in the microwave if necessary. Serve with a scoop of sorbet and Chantilly cream, and place the strawberries around. Spoon some of the balsamic vinegar around and finish with a shard of the black pepper tuile.

A taste of TRADITION

A pub for more than 400 years, The Swan and Talbot in Wetherby has a long history of serving up locally sourced food – one which it continues to this day.

Welcoming people through its doors for more than four centuries, the Swan & Talbot was once a posting inn on the Great North Road. Equidistant from Edinburgh and London, Wetherby has been hosting travelling guests for hundreds of years. Today, however, people are staying for much more than just a passing visit.

The Swan & Talbot stands proudly on North Street in the centre of Wetherby and is becoming known for its locally sourced, seasonal dishes. Awarded the Yorkshire Life Traditional Pub of 2016 award, the Swan & Talbot continues to impress customers and is going from strength to strength among visitors and locals alike.

On the menu, tasty British pub classics with a modern makeover are joined by contemporary dishes delighting diners taste buds. Proud to champion local produce, the Swan & Talbot receives its daily delivery of the freshest produce from a local butcher and fishmonger, as well as Mike the local greengrocer who walks from his nearby shop with his boxes of fresh fruit and vegetables on his shoulders every morning. Working closely with local suppliers, means that the Swan & Talbot can serve up the best and freshest dishes every day, as it has the bounty of Yorkshire's natural larder at its finger tips.

Inside, the pub has low ceilings, befitting of its age, a snug area perfect for an afternoon catch up or an evening drink, and a restaurant which offers breakfast, lunch and dinner. There's also the additional benefit of four letting rooms, where guests are able to stay the night, have a lie in and enjoy a full English breakfast the next morning.

To go alongside their award-winning, enticing wine list, the Swan & Talbot serves a selection of Yorkshire ales, from within a 25-mile radius of Wetherby. So every pint they pull is perfectly prepared and comes from some fantastic local producers. A taste of Yorkshire really does run through everything they do!

The Swan & Talbot
GREEN TEA PANNA COTTA

Served with spiced sticky toffee, candied walnuts and tea-soaked raisins. We also like to accompany this with our white chocolate and popcorn ice cream. This is a dessert that will wow any guests.

Preparation time: 1 hour, plus overnight setting | Cooking time: 45 minutes | Serves 8

Ingredients

For the panna cotta:

200ml whole milk

200ml double cream

100g caster sugar

2 green tea bags

4 gelatine leaves

For the sticky toffee:

300g dates, chopped

150g sultanas

1 tsp bicarbonate of soda

375ml real ale

400g butter

400g dark brown sugar

4 eggs

400g self-raising flour

1 tsp ground ginger

1 tsp ground nutmeg

1 tsp ground cinnamon

For the candied walnuts:

150g sugar

100ml water

250g walnuts

For the sultanas:

500ml black tea

250g sultanas

Method

For the panna cotta

In a saucepan combine the milk, cream, sugar and tea bags. Place on the stove and bring to a simmer. Whilst the liquid is heating soak the gelatine leaves in cold water. When soft and pliable remove them from the water and add to the simmering liquid. Stir in, making sure the gelatine fully dissolves. Pour the mixture through a fine sieve to ensure it is smooth and not contaminated with undissolved gelatine or green tea leaves. Divide the mix between individual dariole moulds or ramekins. Set in the fridge overnight.

For the sticky toffee

Preheat the oven to 180°c. In a saucepan place the dates, sultanas, bicarbonate of soda and real ale. Slowly bring to the boil. Once the fruits are tender, blend until smooth.

In a mixing bowl beat together the butter and sugar until fully creamed. Slowly incorporate the eggs and finally add the flour and spices. Once the mix is smooth slowly add the blended purée. Once fully mixed together, place into a lined baking tin and bake in the oven for 45 minutes until a skewer or small kitchen knife inserted in the centre of the pudding comes out clean.

For the candied walnuts

In a saucepan dissolve the sugar into the water. Do not whisk, stir or tamper with this mix. Place on the heat, and bring to a rapid boil. Leave the solution on the stove top until 30 percent of the pan½½s contents go golden brown. At this stage carefully stir the mix until a is golden brown. Add the walnuts and carefully pour out onto baking parchment to cool. Leave for 20 minutes to come to room temperature then break up the caramel into bite-size pieces and store at room temperature in an airtight container.

For the sultanas

Bring the tea to the boil and pour over the sultanas. Leave for a minimum of 20 minutes to soak before serving.

To serve

Plate up the panna cotta with the sticky toffee pudding and decorate with candied walnuts and tea-soaked sultanas. We serve it with white chocolate and popcorn ice cream.

Life begins AT FORTY

With a history spanning more than 40 years, the award-winning Three Acres has become something of an institution. A place with a far reaching reputation for good food, first-class service and the warmest of welcomes.

Originally established by Derek Truelove in 1968, the inn's ownership subsequently passed down to his son Neil Truelove and business partner Brian Orme, who both share a true passion for food. The mantle has passed today to the next generation, with Neil's son Tom joining them at the helm as partner and chef, securing the third generation in the family business. Tom continues the legacy of this much-loved Yorkshire gem, with his unwavering devotion to the crafting of fine food with the support of general manager Terrence Mackinder. The past forty years have seen numerous developments and growth through various refurbishments to the inn, its accommodation and exclusive private dining areas.

With an array of awards and accolades, the love of food is clearly at the heart of everything they do at The Three Acres. Under the talented leadership of head chef Tom Davies, menus are influenced by an eclectic mix of styles. Expect to see British classics executed beautifully, as well as dishes drawing inspiration from global cuisines – perhaps the collection of menus displayed on the walls acquired from various travels gives a clue as to where the creativity comes from. Only the finest of ingredients produce the very best dishes, so provenance plays a key part in The Three Acres story and the team here have a very keen eye.

Produce coming into the kitchen is either locally farmed, such as meat from Bolster Moor Farm Shop, or has been meticulously sourced for its artisan quality. To this end, the menu feels special and changes to reflect the best of the seasons; always appealing in choice and deliciously presented. There's also an excellent wine list on offer in this cosy inn and the Champagne list tempts with some very fine bottles.

With a dedicated events manager overseeing special celebrations, private events are held in sensational style for all manner of occasions. In addition to the restaurant area, there are several private dining options offered in The Pol Roger Room and The Cattier Tasting Room, allowing guests to dine privately in an elegant setting. The inn has also become a sought-after venue for stylish weddings and often a tipi or two, or a grand marquee can be seen erected in the grounds, all catered with bespoke menus and dedicated waiting staff.

Autographed menus from celebrities, politicians and public figures who have dined at The Three Acres can be spotted adorning the walls. With such a famous client list, discretion is the byword at The Three Acres, but if you fancy dropping in by helicopter, as often clients do, the aviation co-ordinates can be found on their website.

The Three Acres
FRENCH ONION SOUP

This soup has featured on our menu for years and has a bit of a cult following here at the Acres. The truth is that the process takes about 3 days to complete as this whole soup relies heavily on the stock. We turn our French onion stock twice to ensure a great flavour. We also add half onions that we caramelise on the stove tops, this helps both the flavour and the finished colour of the soup.

Preparation time: 30 minutes | Cooking time: 2 hours | Serves 8

Ingredients

1kg white onions, thinly sliced

2 litre beef or veal stock, rich and well flavoured

80g salted butter

Olive oil

150ml Cognac

1 star anise

1 bay leaf

A small loaf sourdough bread, sliced, for croutons

400g Gruyère cheese

Salt and pepper

Method

For the croutons

Begin by drizzling the olive oil on to a large, solid baking-sheet. Add a pinch of salt then, using your hands, spread the oil and salt all over the baking sheet. Now place the bread slices on top of the oil. Turn over each one so that both sides have been lightly coated with the oil.

Bake the bread in the oven for 20-25 minutes until crispy and crunchy.

For the soup

Place a saucepan or casserole dish on the hob on a high heat and melt two tablespoons of oil and butter together. When this is very hot, add the onions and keep turning them from time to time until the edges of the onions have turned dark – this will take about 10 minutes.

Then reduce the heat to its lowest setting and leave the onions to carry on cooking very slowly for 40 minutes to 1 hour, by which time the base of the pan will be covered with a rich, nutty-brown, caramelised layer.

Take off the heat and add the Cognac, ideally try to light the Cognac to burn off the raw alcohol flavour. Allow the mixture to stand for 15 minutes, then proceed to give the onions a good stir; the time standing will help lift all the flavour from off the bottom of the pan. Stir the onions until they are evenly coloured.

Now pour in the rich beef stock, add the star anise and the bay leaf and season with salt and pepper.

As soon as this mix reaches simmering point, turn down the heat to its lowest setting and leave it to cook very gently, without a lid, for a minimum of 1 hour.

To serve

Warm an oven-proof high-sided soup bowl, fill with the hot soup and add a baked sourdough crouton on top. Liberally cover this with grated Gruyère cheese and place the bowls on a tray and finish in the oven or under the grill until the cheese is golden brown and bubbling.

The Three Acres
PRESSED BELLY PORK AND BLACK PUDDING TERRINE

This terrine needs preparing the day before you wish to serve it, but it makes an impressive dinner party starter; worth the wait.

Preparation time: 12 hours-overnight | Cooking time: 30 minutes | Serves 12

Ingredients

For the terrine:

1 side belly pork, skinned and retained for the garnish

2 garlic bulbs

1 stick good quality black pudding

500g duck fat

1 bunch thyme

Vegetable oil

Salt and pepper

For the garnish:

1 side pork skin

2 Granny Smith apples

200g caster sugar

300ml apple juice

1 tsp Cajun spice mix

1 head frisee lettuce

Method

Preheat the oven to 185°c and line a 30cm terrine mould with 3 layers of cling film.

For the terrine

Place the side of belly pork and garlic into a deep baking tray and cover it with the duck fat. Cook this slowly in the oven overnight for 12 hours. Tip: Pour enough duck fat over the pork so when you push down the duck fat comes to the surface. Once cooked, lift the belly pork out of the duck fat and place on a cooling rack.

Place the black pudding into a food processor and blitz until it's soft.

Strip the belly pork into long strands with your hands and chop the thyme. Mix these together, adding salt and pepper to taste along with the confit garlic.

Start layering the terrine into a cling filmed mould, with 1cm layers starting with the belly pork, then black pudding until you have 4 layers of belly pork and 3 layers of black pudding ending with the belly pork.

Fold over the cling film and prick with a knife to let any extra duck fat escape.

Place in the fridge with a suitable weight covering the whole terrine and leave to set.

For the garnish

Place the pork skin in a large pan and cover with water. Weigh the pork down with a plate to keep it submerged. Bring to the boil and cook for about 1-1½ hours or until the skin is soft but not falling apart (adding more water if needed).

Once cooked, carefully remove and place on a cooling rack making sure the skin is in an even layer with no folds. Place in the fridge to cool for about 2 hours or completely cold.

Once the skin is cold, remove any excess fat from the underside, being careful not to tear the pork skin. Place the cooling rack on a tray and cook in the oven overnight with the pork belly to dehydrate the skin until it is dry and brittle.

Snap the skin into 2½cm square pieces. Heat about 10cm of vegetable oil in a deep-sided pan, place one square piece of the skin at a time in the pan and fry it until it turns crispy and puffs up. This takes about 15 seconds. Once cooked, remove from the oil and place onto a paper towel lined tray and season with the Cajun spice while hot.

Finely dice the Granny Smith apples. Place the apple juice and sugar in a pan and cook until reduced and sticky. Add the diced apple and cook until the apple is soft.

To serve

Remove the terrine from the mould and slice into 1½cm slices. Add a small amount of vegetable oil to a frying pan and gently fry the terrine slices until they turn a golden colour on both sides. Arrange on a plate the terrine, apple chutney and pork crackling and garnish with the frisee salad.

The Three Acres
CÔTE DE BOEUF WITH PEPPERCORN OR BÉRNAISE SAUCE

Due to the size of these steaks, it is of great importance to allow the meat to come up to room temperature before cooking, especially if the meat is to be served rare or medium-rare. Allow at least an hour for this, it makes a real difference.

Preparation time: 1 hour to allow the meat to reach room temp | Cooking time: 20 minutes | Serves 4

Ingredients

For the steak:

1kg Côtes de Boeuf

Maldon sea salt

Cracked black pepper

Olive oil

For the peppercorn sauce:

1 small white onion, finely diced

1 small jar green peppercorns in brine, drained

50ml brandy

200ml beef stock

250ml double cream

Worcestershire sauce

Salt and cracked black pepper

For the Bérnaise sauce

2 tbsp white wine vinegar

3 tbsp tarragon, finely chopped, stalks retained

1 small shallot, sliced

10 peppercorns

4 large eggs, yolks only

250g clarified butter (melted butter with milk solids removed)

½ lemon, juiced

Salt

Cayenne pepper

2 tbsp water

Method

For the steak

Heat a grill or griddle pan to a high heat and preheat the oven to 200°c (the meat is far too large to cook all the way on the grill).

Season the steaks with a liberal amount of sea salt and cracked black pepper.

Sear the steaks for 3-4 minutes on both sides, turning 90° half way through to create a criss-cross of char lines.

Transfer the steaks to a roasting tray and place into the oven for 8-10 minutes for medium-rare (depending on thickness).

For the peppercorn sauce

In a saucepan, sweat the diced onion in a little olive oil for 2-3 minutes until softened. Add the drained peppercorns and cook for a further 2 minutes.

Add the brandy and flambé (being careful to keep well back when the alcohol ignites). Once the flames have subsided, add a couple of dashes of Worcestershire sauce to the pan, along with the beef stock. Bring this mixture to the boil and reduce it by half.

Pour in the cream and bring back to the boil. Simmer for 2-3 minutes then season with salt and a generous amount of freshly cracked black pepper.

For the Bérnaise sauce

In a small saucepan, combine the white wine vinegar, shallot, peppercorns and retained tarragon stalks. Bring this mixture to the boil and reduce it by half, then set it aside to cool.

In a mixing bowl, add the cooled vinegar reduction to the egg yolks along with a small splash of cold water, approximately two tablespoons.

Sit the bowl above a saucepan of gently simmering water and whisk the egg mixture constantly. The egg mixture should increase in volume and become thick and silky. Tip: do not allow the egg mixture to get too hot, otherwise it will become scrambled egg!

At this point, remove the egg mixture from the heat and slowly whisk the butter into the mix until all the butter has been emulsified.

Finally add the chopped tarragon and lemon juice, then season with salt and cayenne pepper.

Shipley's hidden
TREASURE

On the bank of the Leeds-Liverpool canal, The Waterside Restaurant & Bar serves modern British cuisine in a historic canal-side building.

Dating from 1875, the building that is home to The Waterside Restaurant & Bar remains a bit of a mystery to its current owners, since no records remain from its early days. Coal, limestone or grain perhaps? Whatever cargo passed through the building during the canal's heyday (2016 marked 200 years since the canal was completed), today it is home to inventive modern cooking using some of Yorkshire's finest produce.

It is run by Ian Johnson and his son-in-law Paul Huddleston who took over the venue in April 2016. For Ian it was the opportunity to allow his talented chef son-in-law to bring his impressive CV back to Yorkshire and realise a long-awaited dream of running his own kitchen.

From the age of 15, Paul has progressed through some of the world's most celebrated dining establishments. From working for Marco Pierre White at The Criterion he then worked under Brian Turner, and it was Brian Turner who then advised him to go and learn the classics in France. These wise words took him to the kitchen of Alain Ducasse's world-famous three Michelin star restaurant Le Louis XV in Monaco. Today, he has brought that incredible wealth of experience back to Shipley.

Paul, a Leeds lad born and bred, describes one of his greatest lessons in France as the commitment to using local produce. The chefs were so passionate about seeking out the very best produce from their region and turning it into stunning dishes, he was inspired to bring this approach to Shipley and now champions local produce in his home county of West Yorkshire.

Freshly caught fish from Hodgson's of Hartlepool, locally grown veg from Delifresh in Bradford and locally reared and completely traceable meat from Bentley's of Pudsey, everything is sourced from within 60 miles of the restaurant.

It's not just local food that is championed at The Waterside Restaurant & Bar. English wine and Yorkshire gin is also popular, along with hand-crafted ales from Saltaire Brewery who are based in Shipley and have more than 70 awards to their name. The two Shipley businesses have nurtured a good friendship and The Waterside is really proud to support their local brewery who have helped to put their town on the world beer map.

Saltaire Brewery, who have been crafting beers since 2006, are best known for their Saltaire Blonde, which is a permanent ale on bars across Yorkshire. However they also create a range of bottled and kegged beers, including seasonal and special beers.

Their relationship with Saltaire Brewery goes hand-in-hand with the homely feel, beautiful views and focus on local food to ensure The Waterside really is a place where the taste of Yorkshire runs through everything they do.

The Waterside Restaurant
DUO OF SHIPLEY HOGGET

Hogget shepherd's pie, herb-rolled cannon of hogget with Saltaire ale jus.

Preparation time: 15 minutes | Cooking time: 4 hours 15 minutes | Serves 4

Ingredients

For the lamb jus:

Lamb bones

½ onion, roughly chopped

1 carrot, roughly chopped

1 stick celery, roughly chopped

A good splash of Saltaire Blonde Ale

A good splash of red wine

For the shepherd's pie:

1kg hogget mince

½ large onion, finely diced

1 carrot, finely diced

2 sticks of celery, diced

1 sprig thyme, chopped

A splash of Saltaire Blond Ale

A splash of red wine

1kg potatoes (Roosters)

For the hogget fillet:

4 x 160g hogget fillet

Dijon mustard, for brushing

A handful of parsley, mint and chives, finely chopped

Blanched spinach, to serve

Method

For the lamb jus

Roast some lamb bones until golden. In a separate pan sweat the roughly chopped onion, carrot and celery. Before the vegetables colour, add the lamb bones, cover with water and simmer for 3 hours.

Reduce the Saltaire ale and red wine by half. Strain the stock into another pan, discard the bones and reduce by half. Add the two reductions together and reduce again by one-third. Season to taste to produce the Saltaire lamb jus.

For the shepherd's pie

Preheat the oven to 140°c. Seal the hogget mince in a frying pan in batches and drain the excess fat. In a separate pan with a little of the hogget fat fry the finely diced onion, carrot, celery and thyme but do not colour. Add the hogget mince and deglaze with a little Saltaire ale and red wine. Cook slowly in the oven for 4 hours until tender.

Peel the potatoes and chop into equal-sized pieces. Cook them in a pan of boiling salted water until soft, then drain and mash.

Take the mince out of the oven, transfer to individual ovenproof dishes or one large ovenproof dish. Top off with mashed potatoes, then bake until the mashed potato topping is crispy.

For the hogget fillet

Seal the hogget all over in a hot pan, brush with Dijon mustard and roll in the chopped herbs. Bake in the oven for 3-4 minutes (depending on size). Leave to rest for 10 minutes somewhere warm.

To serve

Carve the hogget into nice sized slices. Lay on a bed of blanched spinach. Add a portion of the shepherd's pie or individual pot. Finish off with the Saltaire lamb jus.

Escape to the COUNTRY

The White Swan is a traditional Yorkshire pub that oozes charm and character in the gorgeous surroundings of the picturesque village of Wighill.

At the heart of the village, Wighill's pub is a traditional place where food, beer and community come together. The pub also welcomes guests from around the county, thanks to its reputation for transforming local produce into delicious dishes.

Traditional flavours and modern twists go hand in hand at The White Swan. The chefs have built the menu around the very best local ingredients from farms, suppliers and producers close to Wighill. Being surrounded by Yorkshire's stunning countryside means that they have access to some of the region's finest produce, as well as food from just outside of the county. Meat and poultry come from Sykes House Farm, Thorp Arch, fruit and vegetables from Hebden and Poole Fine Foods, and fresh fish is sourced from Hodgson's of Hartlepool.

From sharing boards and snacks to main courses and salads, local produce and fresh, homemade fare is at the centre of everything that comes out of the kitchen. The local platter is a firm favourite – it comprises hand-made stand pie, York ham, pease pudding, home-cured pastrami, piccalilli and Fountains Gold cheddar cheese. Other popular menu classics include the homemade black pudding (which is served with delicious belly pork), Yorkshire rib-eye steak and Blue Wensleydale fritters.

An outside pizza oven provides an enticing new dimension to the menu – it is incredibly popular on Bank Holidays and local festivals, plus is a favourite for private functions taking place at the pub.

The menu is accompanied by the finest Yorkshire cask ales, a carefully selected wine list and lagers and spirits from around the world.

Wighill has a park with a number of countryside walks running through it and the surrounding area, so The White Swan has become a popular spot for ending a countryside stroll. What better way to finish a walk than with a plate of delicious, freshly made food and a pint of locally brewed ale?

The White Swan

THE WHITE SWAN
WIGHILL

The White Swan
MONKFISH WITH WILTED SPINACH, HOLLANDAISE AND POACHED EGG

This is a medley of classic flavours that marry together for comfort food perfection at The White Swan. You will have plenty of hollandaise left over for more portions.

Preparation time: 30 minutes | Cooking time: 20 minutes | Serves 1

Ingredients

For the hollandaise:

50ml white wine vinegar

4 black peppercorns

250g butter, unsalted

4 egg yolks

For the spinach:

1 knob of butter

Good handful of spinach leaves

For the monkfish:

225g monkfish

Oil, for cooking

Salt and ground black pepper

To serve:

1 egg

Boiled baby potatoes

Method

For the hollandaise

Pour the white wine vinegar into a pan, add the black peppercorns, set over a medium heat and reduce by half.

Whilst that is reducing, soften the butter until just melted. Put the yolks into a bowl. Gradually pour over the melted butter, whisking all the time. When all the butter is incorporated, add the reduced vinegar, whisking continuously. (If at this point the sauce splits, it is because it is too hot. The addition of an ice cube or two will bring it back.) Leave the finished sauce to sit at room temperature.

For the spinach

In a sauté pan, melt the butter in a little water, then add the fresh spinach leaves. Stir around gently for 30 seconds to let them wilt. Set aside and keep warm.

For the monkfish

Preheat the oven to 200°c. Season the monkfish with sea salt and freshly ground black pepper, and sear in hot oil in an ovenproof pan for 2 minutes, turning once. After 2 minutes, transfer the pan to the hot oven and leave the fish to bake for 10-15 minutes, depending on the thickness of the fish. When the fish is cooked, remove it from the oven.

To serve

Poach the egg to your liking. Arrange the spinach on a plate, place the monkfish on top and mask with the hollandaise. Finish off with the poached egg on top of the dish. Serve with baby potatoes.

The DIRECTORY

These great businesses have supported the making of this book; please support and enjoy them.

Bolster Moor Farm Shop
Harden Road Farm
1a Bolster Moor Road
Golcar
Huddersfield HD7 4JU
Telephone: 01484 648274
Website:
www.bolstermoorfarmshop.co.uk
Family farm shop, coffee shop and butcher bringing you good food at affordable prices. Champion!

Bondgate Bakery
30 Bondgate
Otley
LS21 1 AD
Telephone: 01943 467516
Website: www.bondgatebakery.com
Baking bread the traditional way since 1984, Bondgate Bakery make all of their products on site from family recipes.

The Box Tree
35-37 Church Street,
Ilkley, West Yorkshire,
LS29 9DR
Telephone: 01943 608484
Website: www.theboxtree.co.uk
An iconic Michelin-starred restaurant set in a charming sandstone cottage in Ilkley. Cooking is refined and skilful, with a classical French base.

Brown's Greens
3b Harrogate Road
Rawdon LS19 6HW
Telephone: 0113 2391489
Website: brownsgreens.co.uk
Vegetarian and vegan café/bistro, with themed menu nights and family events.

Bundobust
6 Mill Hill
Leeds LS1 5DQ
Telephone: 0113 2431248
Website: www.bundobust.com
Indian street food and craft beer.

Buon Apps
Wharfebank Business Centre
Ilkley Road
Otley
West Yorkshire
LS21 3JP
Telephone: 01943 468458
Website: www.buonappsotley.co.uk
Buon Apps brings you the authentic taste of Italy in the heart of Yorkshire. Serving regional specialities from rustic pasta dishes to sophisticated classic meat dishes and of course stoned baked pizza.

Café Moor
Kirkgate Market
34 George Street
Leeds
LS2 7HY
Telephone: 0113 2470569
Website: www.cafemoor.co.uk
The finest North African and Middle Eastern street food made from scratch using fresh local produce.

Caravanserai
1 Crown Street
Leeds
LS2 7DA
Telephone: 0113 2341999
Website: www.caravanseraileeds.co.uk
We serve Ottoman food to inspire and delight the senses. Sit back and relax and take a break from the world with your fellow travellers.

Crafthouse
Level 5 Trinity Leeds
70 Boar Lane
Leeds
LS1 6HW
Telephone: 0113 8970444
Website:
www.crafthouse-restaurant.com
Sleek, industrial-look modern restaurant serving a British menu, chargrilled dishes and fine wines.

Angelica

Level 6 Trinity Leeds
70 Boar Lane
Leeds
LS1 6HW
Telephone: 0113 8970099
Website: www.angelica-restaurant.com
Brasserie dining and cocktails in a stylish, modern, sixth-floor restaurant with a terrace.

Crust and Crumb

110B Harrogate Road
Leeds
LS7 4NY
Telephone: 0113 2680098
Website:
www.crustandcrumbbakery.co.uk
Based in the heart of Chapel Allerton we strive to provide our customers with a friendly, warm atmosphere and give you an experience you will enjoy.

Cryer & Stott

Market Place
Carlton Street
Castleford
WF10 1EB
Telephone: 01977 518371
Website: www.cryerandstott.co.uk

Market Place
Pontefract
WF8 1AU
Telephone: 01977 599744
Website: www.cryerandstott.co.uk
A family run cheesemongers and purveyors of fine foods.

Samuel Valentine Urban Food Hall
20-24 Station Road
Allerton Bywater
Castleford
WF10 2BP
Telephone: 01977 510638
Website: www.cryerandstott.co.uk/samuelvalentine.html
Samuel Valentine combines an attractive blend of superb Yorkshire produce with an emphasis on supporting small local producers and our core values of food and family.

Fazenda

Watermans Place
3 Wharf Approach
Leeds LS1 4GL
Telephone: 0113 4001183
Website: www.fazenda.co.uk
Fazenda Rodizio Bar & Grill – a unique dining experience.

House of Koko

62 Harrogate Road
Chapel Allerton
Leeds
LS7 4LA
Telephone: 0113 2621808
Website: www.houseofkoko.com
Drop in for a coffee and a chat anytime that we're open. We're not pretentious, we love a good gossip and a natter.

Hyde Park Book Club

27-29 Headingley Lane
Leeds LS6 1BZ
Telephone: 0113 3455820
0798 444 9361
Website: www.hydeparkbookclub.co.uk
Coffee, arts, music, books, food, beers, wine, performance and talking space.

Ibérica Leeds

17a East Parade
Hepper House
Leeds LS1 2BH
Telephone: 0113 4037007
Website: www.ibericarestaurants.com
Providing quality Spanish cuisine in a former antique house rich in character and features, at Ibérica Leeds we offer the finest produce served up in a unique menu created by executive chef Nacho Manzano.

Ira B's

27 Chelwood Drive
Leeds LS8 2AT
Telephone: 0113 2302200
Website: www.ira-bs.co.uk
Classic Jewish food, with a slightly bonkers mood.

Jameson's Café and Tea Rooms

647 Roundhay Road
Leeds LS8 4BA
Telephone: 0113 2406688
Website: www.jamesonstearooms.co.uk
A family-run business renowned for wonderful afternoon tea, home-baked cakes, delightful lunches and welcoming atmosphere.

Kirkstall Brewery

100 Kirkstall Road
Leeds LS3 1HJ
Website:
www.kirkstallbrewerycompany.com
The new Kirkstall Brewery situated on the side of the Leeds Liverpool canal and in the shadow of the original brewery.

Kirkstall Bridge Inn

12 Bridge Road
Kirkstall
Leeds LS5 3BW
Telephone: 0113 2784044
Website: www.kirkstallbridge.co.uk
Awarded 'Best Pub in Leeds' three times.

Metcalfe's Butchers

28 Northgate
Cleckheaton
BD19 5AE
Telephone: 01274 874373
Website:
www.metcalfes-butchers.co.uk
A traditional pork and beef family butchers, famous for their stand pies and award-winning bacon.

Mill Kitchen

1 The Old Combing
Sunny Bank Mills
Farsley
LS28 5UJ
Telephone: 0113 2571417
Website: www.millkitchen.co.uk
Relaxed café/deli for brunch, lunch, coffee and cake, we are friendly to vegetarians, vegans, gluten-free folk, bicycles, dogs and children.

Moody Cow
Apperley Lane
Apperley Bridge
Bradford
BD10 0NS
Telephone: 0113 2391444
Website: www.moodycowgrill.co.uk/
apperley-bridge

1-2 New Brook Street
Ilkley
LS29 8DQ
Telephone: 01943 602030
Website:
www.moodycowgrill.co.uk/ilkley
*A steakhouse, bar and grill who source and
serve the finest locally grown, raised and
reared produce.*

Mr Nobody
163 Lower Briggate
Leeds
LS1 6LY
Telephone: 0113 2467013
Website: www.mrnobody.co.uk
*Varied international tasting-style menus
in a sleek, candlelit space with a unique
cocktail list.*

Northern Monk Brew Co.
The Old Flax Store
Marshalls Mill, Holbeck
Leeds LS11 9YJ
Telephone: 0113 2436430 (Brewery)
Telephone: 0113 2430003
(The Refectory and Chapter Hall)
Website:
www.northernmonkbrewco.com
*A forward-thinking brewery that
devotes their passion to crafting beers of
timeless quality and character, all while
aspiring to become the beating heart of the
communities they serve.*

Out of the Woods
Unit B Watermans Place
Granary Wharf
Leeds
LS1 4GL
Telephone: 0113 2454144
Website: www.outofthewoods.me.uk

Out of the Woods
113 Water Lane
Leeds
LS11 5WD
Telephone: 0113 2448123
Website: www.outofthewoods.me.uk
*We pride ourselves on creating exciting,
healthy and delicious food and drinks
with an emphasis on using fantastic local
suppliers.*

ProperMaid
Bank Bottom Works
Marsh Garden
Huddersfield
West Yorkshire
HD9 6AP
Telephone: 01484 766068
Website: www.propermaid.co.uk
*We make uniquely fabulous 'proper' cakes
and baked products that are competitively
priced and supported by friendly,
professional service.*

The Queen o' t' owd Thatch
101 High Street
South Milford LS25 5AQ
Telephone: 01977 685096
Website: www.theqott.com
*Yorkshire dining pub – drinker, diner and
dog friendly, we use Yorkshire produce
for our seasonal menus, serve a fabulous
Sunday lunch and excellent wines,
cocktails and well-kept cask ales.*

Saltaire Brewery Limited
The Brewery
County Works, Dockfield Road
Shipley BD17 7AR
Telephone: 01274 594959
Website: www.saltairebrewery.co.uk
*International award-winning brewery,
brewing hand crafted ales since 2006.*

Stockdales of Yorkshire
8 South Parade
Leeds LS1 5QX
Telephone: 0113 2042460
Website:
www.stockdales-restaurant.com
*Stockdales is a premium British steakhouse
dedicated to combining the finest local
produce with excellent culinary skill
to provide a truly memorable dining
experience.*

Swan & Talbot
30 North Street
Wetherby LS22 6NN
Telephone: 01937 582040
Website: www.swanandtalbot.com
*The Swan & Talbot has been a feature of
Wetherby for over 400 years and continues
to offer Yorkshire cask ales, locally sourced
food and award-winning warm and
friendly service.*

The Three Acres
Roydhouse
Shelley
Nr Huddersfield
West Yorkshire
HD8 8LR
Telephone: 01484 602606
Website: www.3acres.com
*Join The Three Acres for a feast made of
fine Yorkshire and artisan ingredients.*

Tim Green Photography
8 Church Lane
Tingley
Wakefield WF3 1BQ
Telephone: 07768 305059
Website:
www.timgreenphotographer.co.uk
*West Yorkshire-based photographer,
specialising in studio and location.*

The Waterside Restaurant & Bar
Unit B, Wharf Street
Shipley
West Yorkshire BD17 7DW
Telephone: 01274 594444
Website:
www.waterside-restaurant.co.uk
*Nestled on the banks of the Leeds
Liverpool canal, The Waterside Restaurant
& Bar offers you fine dining at an
affordable price.*

The White Swan
Main Street
Wighill LS24 8BQ
Telephone: 01937 832217
Website:
www.thewhiteswanwighill.co.uk
*A traditional Yorkshire pub oozing charm
and character in the picturesque village of
Wighill serving cask ales, fine wines and
the freshest locally sourced food.*

Other titles in the 'Get Stuck In' series

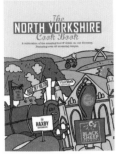

The North Yorkshire Cook Book
features Andrew Pern, Visit York, Made in Malton, Black Sheep Brewery and lots more.
978-1-910863-12-1

The Birmingham Cook Book
features Glynn Purnell, The Smoke Haus, Loaf Bakery, Simpsons and lots more.
978-1-910863-10-7

The Bristol Cook Book
features Dean Edwards, Lido, Clifton Sausage, The Ox, and wines from Corks of Cotham plus lots more.
978-1-910863-14-5

The Oxfordshire Cook Book
features Mike North of The Nut Tree Inn, Sudbury House, Jacobs Inn, The Muddy Duck and lots more.
978-1-910863-08-4

The Lancashire Cook Book
features Andrew Nutter of Nutters Restaurant, Bertram's, The Blue Mallard and lots more.
978-1-910863-09-1

The Liverpool Cook Book
features Burnt Truffle, The Art School, Fraiche, Villaggio Cucina and many more.
978-1-910863-15-2

The Sheffield Cook Book - Second Helpings
features Jameson's Tea Rooms, Craft & Dough, The Wortley Arms, The Holt, Grind Café and lots more.
978-1-910863-16-9

The Derbyshire Cook Book
features Chatsworth Estate, Fischer's of Baslow, Thornbridge Brewery and lots more.
978-0-9928981-7-5

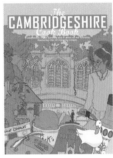

The Cambridgeshire Cook Book
features Daniel Clifford of Midsummer House, The Pint Shop, Gog Magog Hills, Clare College and lots more.
978-0-9928981-9-9

The Suffolk Cook Book
features Jimmy Doherty of Jimmy's Farm, Gressingham Duck and lots more.
978-1-910863-02-2

The Manchester Cook Book
features Aiden Byrne, Simon Rogan, Harvey Nichols and lots more.
978-1-910863-01-5

The Lincolnshire Cook Book
features Colin McGurran of Winteringham Fields, TV chef Rachel Green, San Pietro and lots more.
978-1-910863-05-3

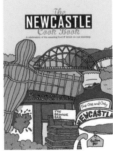

The Newcastle Cook Book
features David Coulson of Peace & Loaf, Bealim House, Grainger Market, Quilliam Brothers and lots more.
978-1-910863-04-6

The Cheshire Cook Book
features Simon Radley of The Chester Grosvenor, The Chef's Table, Great North Pie Co., Harthill Cookery School and lots more.
978-1-910863-07-7

The Leicestershire & Rutland Cook Book features Tim Hart of Hambleton Hall, John's House, Farndon Fields, Leicester Market, Walter Smith and lots more.
978-0-9928981-8-2

All books in this series are available from Waterstones, Amazon and independent bookshops.

FIND OUT MORE ABOUT US AT WWW.MEZEPUBLISHING.CO.UK